T0129189

SANE DRIVING
in a
MAD WORLD

SANE DRIVING
in a
MAD WORLD

DRIVING SAFETY, COURTESY, AND RESPONSIBILITY

ROBERT W. BOXER, M.D.

SANE DRIVING IN A MAD WORLD
DRIVING SAFETY, COURTESY, AND RESPONSIBILITY

iUniverse books may be ordered through booksellers or by contacting:

iUniverse
1663 Liberty Drive
Bloomington, IN 47403
www.iuniverse.com
1-800-Authors (1-800-288-4677)

ISBN: 978-1-5320-1009-5 (sc)
ISBN: 978-1-5320-1008-8 (e)

Library of Congress Control Number: 2016918069

Print information available on the last page.

iUniverse rev. date: 05/24/2017

CONTENTS

DISCLAIMER

Sane Driving in a Mad World is intended to reduce the chance of a crash or other unfortunate incident, however, the author and publisher can assume no liability or responsibility, since there are so many variables involved. *Sane Driving in a Mad World* does not provide driver education, or driver training, but is intended to provide information regarding the author's observations and interest, and relevant experiences, opinions, and references concerning driving safety.

Although an effort has been made to insure the accuracy of this book, it may still contain typographical and/or content or judgment errors, and therefore should be used as a general guide. Cars, techniques, as well as laws, and even individual skills are subject to change in the future.

This book will not likely cover all possible scenarios or situations that can be encountered. Readers are therefore urged to give thought to the advice contained within, and to modify or even disregard that advice when necessary for individual situations that may still present a unique opportunity, but also a necessity, to make a different, perhaps even entirely new decision on how to act.

If any suggestions in this book do not seem to fit your experience or judgment, or you see a different way in which you could or should react, consult with a drivers-ed specialist, the local police, and even at times run your thoughts by an experienced respected adult driver.

All readers must accept the lack of liability on the part of the author and publisher of this book, and therefore consequently they must assume personal responsibility for their actions. If they are not able to do this, then I urge them not to read *Sane Driving in a Mad World.*

DEDICATION

Sane Driving in a Mad World is dedicated to the memory of my late father, Isadore Boxer, who along with my driver's education teacher, the late Mr. W. Roy Means, at Southwest High School in Kansas City, Missouri, taught me how to drive. My father set a great example for courtesy and responsibility as well as safety. He always said, "It doesn't cost anymore to be nice to people." This book is also dedicated to Jesse White, the outstanding long-serving Illinois Secretary of State, who along with the *Chicago Tribune*, did an extensive study and expose' of the problems with teenage drivers, leading to a more demanding, and widely acclaimed graduated licensing law in the State of Illinois. The Secretary of State has also been involved in many other efforts to enhance safety for drivers in the State of Illinois. This book is also dedicated to the millions of responsible drivers who make an effort to be courteous and safe and to respect the rights and safety of other drivers, passengers, motorcyclists, bicyclists and pedestrians. Last, but certainly not least, this book is also dedicated to the law enforcement officers who serve and protect, firemen, ambulance drivers and paramedics, the highway construction workers, and the State Department of Transportation "Minute Men" truck drivers who patrol the expressways and assist motorists in need, all of whom put their lives on the line to make our driving experience safer.

FOREWORD

I HAVE ALWAYS BEEN INTERESTED IN DRIVING safety. As a physician, I read books
and articles by orthopedic surgeons, neurosurgeons, pediatricians, public
health officials, and family practitioners, about the horrendous toll both in lives
lost, and pain, suffering, and time lost due to injuries from auto accidents. Early
in my medical career, I was a member of Physicians for Automotive Safety.

Between internship and residency, I took a year off to work as a physician.
At that time, driving to and from work, I observed people changing tires
on the side of the road, or being involved in other emergencies where they
were obviously endangered. Because of that, I conceived of, and applied
for a patent on a "Traffikone," an emergency highway marker for disabled
cars (drivers who needed to change tires, and deal with other emergencies).
This was a water resistant fiberboard, red and yellow striped pyramid,
with reflective coating on the top four inches. Two spreader bars placed at
different heights in the base were used to stabilize it and weight it down.
It folded flat. I, and two friends who joined in the venture, sold several
thousand Traffikones before all three of us became too involved in our own
main careers. While an internal medicine resident at Cook County Hospital
in Chicago, in the little spare time that I had, I designed and installed in my
1960 Chevrolet, a relay and buzzer that would alert a driver if the headlights
were left on after the engine was turned off. It worked. A physician colleague
was planning to present this to General Motors, but he took a residency
in another area and we didn't pursue this further. Several years later, auto
on/off switches were built into cars, and automatic turn off of lights was
incorporated into the newer switches. I take absolutely no credit for this.

As a physician who had been well trained at the Feinberg School of
Medicine of Northwestern University, Cook County Hospital, and the
University of Illinois College of Medicine, I felt an obligation to assist
motorists who had accidents, or disabled automobiles. I began to put

together a comprehensive kit with emergency equipment that could be used by the driver or car involved in the emergency, and could also be used by a passerby to assist. Although I made a fair amount of progress in that direction, I was bogged down by the responsibilities of a private medical practice and I abandoned the project before completion.

I've written over 100 articles that were published in the "Voice of the People Column" of the *Chicago Tribune,* as well as in local newspapers, such as the Wilmette Life, Wilmette Beacon, and Skokie Life. Many of those were about driving safety. Needless to say, I also submitted articles that were not printed. The *Chicago Tribune* has printed several of my longer articles on items such as *Hazards of Airbags,* and *Unintended Acceleration,* as well as a critical commentary regarding directions for motorists to the nearest trauma center or hospital. This latter extensive commentary led to a television appearance with a trauma nurse, on a local network station.

In 2004, I decided to write a book on driving safety, courtesy, and responsibility. I was noticing many repeated occurrences on the road and analyzing them in a way that I had learned to approach medicine. During the last 12 years, I have read a number of books that were accessible to me in terms of automotive safety. Some of these are mentioned in the section on acknowledgments and references. I would read articles in the AARP and AAA's publications which were often helpful. Blue Cross and Blue Shield of Illinois would send out newsletters periodically that had to do in part with automotive safety. I annually review in detail the current State of Illinois Rules of the Road. I have permission from the Office of Jesse White, the long serving and greatly appreciated Illinois Secretary of State, to reproduce sections of the 2009 and 2013 Rules of the Road, with the condition that I would mention that any aspect could change from year to year. I recommend that all drivers read the current Rules of the Road, ideally every year. I also reviewed the Rules of the Road from a number of other states. Many of these are available online and generally they cover similar circumstances, except for mountainous states which would emphasize safety measures not necessarily applicable to other states. There are a number of websites which give helpful information to drivers and many of these will be listed at the back of *Sane Driving in a Mad World.*

I also gleaned information from television and radio programs, and read the *Chicago Tribune* and *Wall Street Journal,* both of which often carried important information, particularly regarding significant recalls which had major safety implications. I read articles pertaining to automotive safety, and autonomous cars, in BloombergBusinessweek. I spoke with knowledgable friends and relatives. I listen to WBBM radio traffic reports most mornings and frequently during evening rush hours. Driver input to alert Radio Station WBBM of difficult Chicagoland traffic situations is 1-855-780-7623. This change occured in March 2017.

I was the stimulus for, and one of the main members of, a resident's traffic patrol organized in the 1990's under the auspices and supervision of George Carpenter, the former Chief of Police of the Village of Wilmette. The emphasis of this patrol effort was regarding cars that were speeding through school zones in residential streets, often at a time and place where children were going to or coming from school.

The purpose of *Sane Driving in a Mad World* is to point out the unique situations that require some forethought, and mainly have to do with safety, but also importantly involve courtesy and responsibility. The original book on this subject was copyrighted by myself in 2013. That version included a number of personal experiences. In an effort to write in a more concise and direct manner, I have eliminated many of these. My intention is that this is a more readable version which covers the significant points from the earlier version, and is updated.

Driving safety, courtesy and responsibility means being held accountable for the way you drive, the safety and comfort of your passengers and yourself, the integrity and proper maintenance of your car, and the safety of other cars, pedestrians, motorcyclists, and bicyclists that you encounter while driving. This book will briefly touch on some important aspects of maintenance, but does not go into as much detail as other books specifically directed toward auto maintenance.

Sane Driving in a Mad World should be helpful for more experienced drivers, as well as older drivers who would like to become more aware of some of the subtle, less obvious safety and courtesy aspects, possibly those that may not have been covered in the usual adult driver refresher courses. This book would be an ideal book for teenagers and other beginning drivers to read, and in appropriate instances, for the parents of teenagers to also read so that they can set an example at an early age for their teenagers.

Tens of thousands of Americans die each year as a result of accidents involving automobiles. In addition to the deaths on the roads, several million people in this country are injured each year. The huge economic losses, pain and suffering, as well as inconveniences are all mainly preventable, and *that* is the reason for this book.

It is probable that some of the points made in this book will have been presented in other publications and other instructional materials and teaching courses, but many of the points presented have occurred to me in the course of everyday driving, and I have not seen them elsewhere. There also are a number of important points that have been gleaned from various state drivers' manuals, as well as from other sources that will be indicated. Hardly a day goes by that I don't see an additional occurrence which might find a place in future editions.

Much of the advice in this book represents my own observations, as a concerned and analytical driver, even at times as a passenger or pedestrian, along with that which is commonly known to a great extent, and in the public domain. *Sane Driving in a Mad World* is not a textbook, but rather an ancillary book to enable drivers to increase their knowledge of safety measures, courtesy, and responsibility. Originally the subtitle was Common and Uncommon Sense Driving Safety, Courtesy, and Responsibility. This has been shortened to eliminate the Common and Uncommon Sense, something which I hope the readers (drivers) won't do, since *Sane Driving in a Mad World* still represents that.

Sources of information have included: the Insurance Institute for Highway Safety (IIHS); AOL Autos; Edmunds; Mothers Against Drunk Driving (MADD); Students Against Destructive Decisions (SADD); Consumer Reports; publications by AAA (American Automobile Association or "Triple A" as it is often referred to); the American Academy of Orthopedic Surgeons; and the American Academy of Pediatrics as well as some sources mentioned in the Foreword.

I would urge all those with serious interest in driving safety to take advantage of many of the above resources on an ongoing basis.

Although some books have a summary at the end of each chapter, many of the topics and chapters in *Sane Driving in a Mad World* are not only short, but all of the content is important. Summaries are not included for many of these chapters. A number of important points are in a summary at the end, but it is not all-inclusive. Interested, motivated, and dedicated drivers are urged to read the entire *"Sane Driving in a Mad World."*

INTRODUCTION

T HERE ARE SECTIONS ON MANY ASPECTS of the subject matter. Please see the Table of Contents.

Sane Driving in a Mad World is not intended to take the place of formal driving education by qualified instructors, as well as supervision by parents and other qualified adults. It is especially intended to bring up some aspects that may not be mentioned or emphasized in the ordinary courses of instruction.

For those interested in details on high speed maneuvers, sophisticated kidnapping evasion, and other more advanced techniques that are available in some of the other books and driving schools, a reader would be referred to the Internet.

Sane Driving in a Mad World docs assume that the driver has a basic knowledge of the mechanics of driving a car, and has a certain basic level of driving skill, which is an important prerequisite, as are attitudes, perspectives, values, and awareness.

I particularly found featured articles by Jim Mateja, and the column by Bob Weber, both of which have appeared in the *Chicago Tribune*, to be especially useful. I've also reviewed interactive DVDs from AAA, and I took the National Safety Council's Defensive Driver's Course. Consumer Reports is an excellent resource for car reliability, driving safety, and shopping for new and used cars. Edmunds and the Kelley Blue Book are also very useful. Safercar.gov is the website set up by the National Highway Traffic Safety Administration and is something drivers should be familiar with. There are many more websites and resources listed at the end of *Sane Driving in a Mad World*.

The American Automobile Association (AAA as it is often referred to) is an excellent resource for roadside service, as well as various types of insurance, Trip Tix, maps, and many other areas of assistance to drivers, including hotel and rental car discounts. AAA offers many services to teen drivers, including free membership for those whose parents are also members.

Much of the advice in this book represents my own observations recorded as a concerned and analytical driver, and importantly, even at times as a passenger or pedestrian. Although my efforts have been especially during the past twelve years, this book encompasses a lifetime of driving, observing and learning.

Most automobile accidents (often more properly labeled crashes, since many of them are due to driver error and therefore are preventable) are due to excessive or inappropriate speed, tailgating (following too closely), use of alcohol or other drugs, distractions, poor driving habits, and not having a plan for the innumerable situations and emergencies that can occur. The increased incidence of serious and even fatal road rage is dealt with in detail.

The Rules of the Road manual for each state can change from year to year. I highly recommend that all drivers review their current state's Rules of the Road or equivalent, and do this on a yearly basis. I also suggest that all drivers review the driver's manual for their cars, especially if they have a new car, or haven't yet had a chance to review this important source of information designed to allow them to become familiar with all the features of their car.

> **One perspective that I have found uniquely helpful, is to look at each situation both ways, i.e. from the point of view of the reader (driver) and from the point of view of the other driver or drivers potentially involved.**

I feel strongly that parents should start instructing teenagers at least several years, if not sooner, before they actually start driving. This assumes that parents would drive safely, courteously, and responsibly, and would point out the reasons that they do or don't do certain things in particular situations. Ideally they should also point out other cars that may be doing the right thing, or in some instances the wrong thing.

I recommend that interested students and drivers read *"The Driving*

Challenge (Dare to be Safer and Happier on the Road)" by Phil Berardelli, and *"Safe Young Drivers (A Guide for Parents and Teens)"* also by Mr. Berardelli. These books were helpful and are highly recommended, particularly in regards to the proper attitude for drivers to acquire. Mr. Berardelli also wrote *"Safe Senior Drivers (A Guide for a Critical Time)."* Although I have not had an opportunity to read this latter book, I would presume it would be as helpful as his other books. The publisher, Nautilus Communications, Inc., P.O. Box 1600, Vienna, VA 22183-1600, and Mr. Berardelli did generously give me permission to refer to any part of his books. By and large however, there are areas that would be better reviewed by also reading those books, which are available through Amazon.com

The term accident, crash, collision, or wreck might be used pretty much interchangeably in the context of this work even though most instances are properly called a "crash." A collision implies striking another vehicle or even an immovable object such as an underpass abutment, or a movable object such as wildlife. A "wreck" can even involve just a single vehicle, such as one which has run off the road and/or overturned. Obviously there can be combinations, i.e. a wreck may involve a collision.

Details of my extensive driving history are presented in the Appendix.

SELECTION OF SAFER CARS

WHILE IN GENERAL, LARGER CARS ARE safer then smaller cars, modern technology has often significantly increased the safety of smaller cars. This includes anti-lock brakes, electronic stability control, traction control, greater use of air bags, and crumple zones. Adaptive cruise control, forward collision alert, automatic emergency braking (AEB) which may become operative at different speeds in different cars, lane drifting alert, blind spot detection, parking assist and back up cameras are also options that are increasingly being offered but sometimes passed up by buyers because of the increased costs. Similar equipped larger cars will still have a safety advantage over smaller cars. While many if not most of these advanced features are helpful, a careful, confident, alert and focused driver is still a major factor in crash avoidance.

Safety testing done by the Insurance Institute for Highway Safety (IIHS), National Highway Traffic Safety Administration (NHTSA), and Consumer Reports are all good resources.

In selecting a used car, it is very important to ask for the Carfax or Auto Check to be sure that cars that have been in crashes or accidents have proper reinstallation of workable airbags. When buying a used car, it is important to not only test drive it, but also to bring it to a trusted mechanic to have it looked over very carefully, especially from the standpoint of safety and to be certain the car has not been damaged in a flood or another weather event. **It is extremely important to know whether or not all recalls have been satisfactorily addressed.**

If buying a used car, try to pick one that is two to four years old that may have some of the more advanced safety features mentioned above, especially electronic stability control, side curtain airbags, ability to use integrated apps, and something which has been around for a while, built in GPS. Also in buying a used car you should look for a good score on the IIHS small overlap test.

Consumer Reports is especially good in terms of evaluating cars for safety and reliability.

Although there may be some advantages, as well as disadvantages, to other types of vehicles, my personal thought is that standard sedans are a better choice for beginners.

Keeping the headlights on at all times has been shown to be a significant safety factor, although perhaps of somewhat less importance since most new cars have daytime running lights, which are small lights on each side of the front of the car which would be on whenever the engine is running. Lighter colored cars, including white cars, have been shown to be more visible and hence less likely to be involved in a crash.

SUMMARY: In general, larger cars are safer then smaller cars, although both may be equipped with advanced safety features, especially electronic stability control, side curtain airbags, forward collision warning, automatic emergency braking, blind spot monitoring, lane departure warning, back-up cameras, ability to use integrated apps, built-in GPS, and adaptive cruise control. If buying a used car, try to pick one that is two to four years old that may have some of the more advanced safety features mentioned.

MIRRORS; REAR VIEW AND SIDE VIEW

It is advisable to have a set pattern of constantly checking your mirrors, including the rear view, left and right side view mirrors, as well as keeping a close eye on what's in front of you. Remember that the right side view mirror will have a warning stating "Objects in mirror are closer then they appear." It is very important to be aware of this perception especially if you are changing lanes to the right, and you should practice this with an instructor.

THE RIGHT PASSENGER SIDE VIEW MIRROR should be adjusted so that sitting in the normal driving position, you see just the slightest sliver of your car, and when a car passing on the right moves out of view from your rear view mirror, it should be visible in the side view mirror. When it is no longer visible in the side view mirror, by turning your head to the right, you should be able to see the car through the window or windows on the right side of your car. Caution: a very short car or motorcycle or any other shorter vehicle may stay hidden in either left or right side blind spots, especially if you have a wide pillar separating the front and rear seat compartments. Cars that are unusually low slung may not always be visible through the side window of a higher vehicle, depending on how the mirror is set.

The left side view mirror should be similarly adjusted so that you see only the slightest sliver of your car and some have suggested not even seeing any of your car in order to minimize the blind spot. Again, when a car moves out of view from your rear view mirror, you should be able to see it in your left side view mirror, and when it leaves that, you should be able to see it by looking out the left (drivers) window or windows. You should look to the rear past the pillar that separates the front and rear seat compartments to be certain to minimize the blind spot on either side.

Your rear view mirror should be set so that you see fully the back window of your vehicle, even though headrests may occupy a portion of the lower view and passengers sitting in the back seat can also impinge upon your view.

It is advisable to have a set pattern of constantly checking your mirrors, both the rear view, left and right side view mirrors as well as keeping a close eye on what's in front of you.

I've found that leaning forward and slightly to the left to check your left side view mirror when changing lanes or merging to the left affords a better view. You have to be careful to not steer in the direction that you move your head, since there is a natural tendency to do that, but most drivers quickly learn to correct that tendency.

When changing lanes at night, be careful that a car or truck is not pulling a trailer, a boat or snowmobile, or for that matter any kind of trailer, especially a low slung one since this may be difficult to see, especially at night. You should always signal when you change lanes even if there are no cars around you and you should develop the habit of always signaling when you change lanes or turn, no matter what the circumstances. Developing that habit insures that you will automatically do the right thing.

It is important to not assume that just because you have signaled that it is safe to change lanes or to merge. You have to be sure there is an opening and I and others often have indicated that it is better to signal *after* you have ascertained an opening. There are times when you may want to change to exit, and by using turn signals, you may want to give cars in the other lane the opportunity to extend courtesy to you by hanging back and allowing you to change lanes.

Constantly monitoring your mirrors helps you automatically and more accurately anticipate other drivers moves. For instance, if a car passes you on the right or left at a high speed, the car in front of it might cut in front of you just to get out of the way of that speeding car, or even just as likely, the speeding car might very well cut in front you. You should automatically anticipate this possibility and adjust your speed (slow down) or lane, to allow for this possibly predictable behavior of other drivers.

You should be looking ahead and scanning the road and surrounding area for at least a few hundred yards for potential road hazards which could include approaching vehicles, pedestrians, animals or other obstacles that might enter your path. This is particularly important if the road is narrow and there is no shoulder, in which case you need to increase your following distance.

The merge sign means speed up if necessary so that you can merge, but that implies that there will be an opening which there isn't always, whereas the yield signs means slow down and even stop if necessary, waiting for an opportunity to safely enter the road that you are intending to enter.

SUMMARY: The side view mirror should be adjusted so that sitting in the normal driving position, you see just the slightest sliver of your car on that side, and when a car is passing you on either side moves out of view from your rear view mirror, it should be visible in the side view mirror. When it is no longer visible in the side view mirror, turning your head to the side involved, you should be able to see the car through the window or windows on that side of your car. You should look to the rear on that side past the pillar that separates the front and rear seat compartments to be sure to minimize the blind spot. Be aware that extremely short cars, motorcycles and bicycles, as well as low slung cars may not always be visible by following the above. You can usually check the proper positioning of the mirrors while you are waiting for a light to change and cars on either side have either an arrow to turn, or they are going straight and passing you as you are waiting to turn.

MOST COMMON CAUSES OF VEHICLE CRASHES

Speeding

SPEEDING, ALONG WITH IMPROPER INTERVAL BETWEEN cars, and driving under the influence of alcohol and/or drugs (including prescription and non-prescription medications), and distractions, are often cited as being among the most common causes of serious and fatal vehicle crashes.

"Velocitization" means getting used to going from a lower speed limit to a higher speed limit, or vice versa. This is probably most important when you are coming into a lower speed zone from an expressway or freeway, and you need to also check ramp speed warning signs or the speed limit signs, and glance at the speedometer to make sure that you have slowed down enough. It is important to slow down before you enter a curve, so that you will ideally not have to brake while in the curve. You may even be able to gently accelerate through the curve, which would give you slightly more traction on the road, especially if dry.

Driver reaction in terms of feet traveled, which therefore means braking distance, also measured in terms of feet traveled, is markedly increased as you increase your speed. On clean, level asphalt pavement, your stopping distance at 30 mph, which would ordinarily be between 110-115 feet, becomes approximately 240 feet at 50 mph, and approximately 415 feet at 70 mph. This means that the faster you are going, the greater the interval should be between you and the car in front of you. The above quoted braking distances are based on a reaction time of 1.5 seconds and that obviously can vary from driver to driver. That also assumes good brakes as well as good tires and straight and dry roads.

A basic rule would be that you must drive at a speed that is reasonable for existing conditions. Remember the higher the speed that you are traveling, the less time you have to identify hazards, judge the speed of other traffic, and react to avoid the inevitable mistakes of other drivers. The basic rule that you must drive at a speed that is reasonable for existing conditions means in relation to other traffic, which would include pedestrians and bicycles, the surface and the width of the road, the presence or absence of shoulders, the hazards at intersections, and very importantly the weather. Fog, rain, snow, wind, and blowing blizzard can affect visibility and traction, as can other conditions that could affect safety.

Posted speed signs help you determine a reasonable and prudent speed for ideal conditions. The basic rule does allow you to drive under the minimum speed limit if conditions dictate that is the only way you can proceed safely. I, as well as most other drivers, have been in heavy snow storms on roads that are meant to be driven on anywhere from 35 to 55 mph or even higher, and cars were understandably creeping along at 5, 10 or 15 mph.

Speeding also reduces a driver's ability to steer around obstacles. Seat belts, airbags, highway guardrails (and hitting some of them head on can result in serious injury or death because of a defect in design), and other safety features are less effective if a driver is speeding. You should utilize all safety features at any speed, but remember at high speeds, all safety features will be less effective.

Alcohol use and racing are also prominent killers of younger drivers, but can affect any age.

A basic rule would be that you must drive at a speed that is reasonable for existing conditions, and this repetition is for emphasis. The faster you are going, the less your chance of controlling the car safely if you have a blowout. For similar reasons it is important to always have two hands on the steering wheel, so that in case of a blowout or other emergency, you are more likely to be able to maintain control of the car.

Remember that driving too slow also creates a difficult and dangerous situation for other drivers, and therefore for yourself. If your driving skills are not adequate for at least the minimum posted speed, then you should avoid being on an expressway or freeway. Actually, even at the minimum speed, a hazard is created since other drivers are almost certain to be weaving in and out to pass you. **Drive with the flow of traffic at a legal**

speed. Stay out of the left lane unless you need to pass other cars. Maintain safe driving habits even if other drivers are speeding or cutting in and out or tailgating.

Interval Between Cars

> **The faster you are going, the greater the interval should be between you and the car in front of you, since distance traveled during reaction time, as well as braking distances, will increase as your speed increases.**

Many state driver's manuals suggest a three second rule at ordinary highway speeds which could be 45-55 mph. In the Chicago area, I would suspect four or even five seconds is more reasonable, since even on the 55 mph expressways, cars are usually going faster. So at speeds of 55, 65 or even 75 mph, the three seconds should really be four, five or even six seconds. This is assuming a good road which is dry, and good brakes, and that you are not tired, or traveling at night. This essentially means that when the car in front of you passes a pole or tree, it should be three seconds (counted one thousand one, one thousand two, one thousand three, etc.) before the front of your car comes to the same marker. Some states have used four second rules and some even two (which might be appropriate in 25 mph zones).

> **Heavy traffic as well as any factor affecting visibility, especially weather, and tiredness could easily increase the time interval between cars that would be reasonable and safe. For *each* condition mentioned, you should *add* at least one additional second.**

Following another car too closely is a major cause of crashes. Keeping a reasonable interval allows you to observe obstacles such as objects that have fallen off of trucks or cars, potholes or other problems in the road, and also gives you the opportunity to see the effect of road conditions on the car in front of you in time to respond appropriately.

Many if not most drivers seem to be overconfident in their ability to react, and this often leads to dangerous tailgating. Tailgating can also incite road rage. It is especially important not to tailgate the car in front of you approaching an intersection where there is a red light camera because the driver is more likely to suddenly put on the brakes if the light is about to change, or changes, in an effort to avoid a ticket. It seems as though the incidence of major crashes has decreased with red light cameras at some intersections, although this is not consistent, but the incidence of rear-end crashes has often increased.

The weight distribution in your car or truck, your suspension and shock absorbers, the direction and speed of the wind, the type, condition, and adjustment of your brakes, the kind, as well as the width, of your tires, and the condition of the tread on your tires as well as the condition of the surface of the road will all impact on braking distances, and **therefore will impact on your reasonable speed and interval behind the car in front of you.** In addition to lessening the odds of a collision, keeping a reasonable interval behind the car in front of you, allows other cars to merge or change lanes, without you having to hit the brakes and possibly cause a chain reaction, creating a traffic jam. This additional reason for an average and steady speed and safe interval was suggested by William J. Beaty, an engineer from Seattle, Washington in an excellent article by Sue Shellenbarger in the Wall Street Journal, page D1-2, October 12 2 016. Mr. Beaty has a website, trafficwaves.org. He points out in the article that his observations about traffic aren't new, traffic experts and long-haul truckers have known this for a long time. Ms. Shellenbarger's article is very informative

> **SUMMARY: You should follow the posted speed limits if conditions are ideal, i.e. a good road which is straight and dry, you have good brakes, and you are not tired. For each adverse condition mentioned in the above, add one second to the three or four second basic rule applying to the interval behind the vehicle in front of you.**

CRASH AVOIDANCE

(Much of this chapter is devoted to left turns at intersections, and to a lesser extent to right turns at intersections, but also to intersections in general since more, if not most, crashes occur at intersections.)

IN RESIDENTIAL NEIGHBORHOODS WHERE THERE MAY be no stop signs or traffic lights, you just have to watch for cars coming in the cross direction. The best suggestion is "covering the brake" just as you are getting to the intersection, so that if you do see something that could result in a crash, you can act to avoid it. Covering the brake means you have your foot on the brake as you approach the intersection, being prepared to stop if necessary. If after entering the intersection, and observing whether there is cross traffic, transferring your foot to the accelerator might allow you to finish crossing the intersection, especially if a car is suddenly noted to be speeding into the intersection from the cross street. This actually is often true even if your path is "protected" by stop signs on the cross street.

Traffic lights or stop signs for cross traffic at an intersection make it a protected intersection. Unfortunately, many drivers run stop signs, sometimes unintentionally. Many drivers are not concentrating or are talking on the phone or texting or listening to the radio, or even talking to passengers, which may lead to sometimes running a stop sign or a red light. It is good to anticipate that this could happen and be prepared to stop, and **always be alert for drivers who might run a stop sign or a red light**.

Driving while intoxicated, or under the influence of alcohol or medication or drugs, speeding, being momentarily distracted, or even falling asleep, can all sometimes contribute to running a red light or stop sign.

Left turns are particular problems, especially at busy intersections, and these are one of the most dangerous turns for several reasons. If you are turning left, you have to be able to judge oncoming traffic, and also be aware of *their* traffic light. Especially be aware that the traffic light *that you are watching for your side may not be exactly timed the same as the opposing traffic light for oncoming traffic.* Don't assume that because you see your light change to caution, that opposing traffic is necessarily going to slow down, when in fact they might have a longer green light or green arrow than you. Sometimes there is a sign to indicate that discrepancy between the timing of the lights, but I've seen more and more intersections where there was no warning or indication of that. You have to be certain that the opposing cars are not only planning to stop, but also are in fact stopping or have stopped. One of the most difficult things for new drivers to learn is how to judge the distance and speed of an oncoming car in this situation. Our brain works in such a way that as the image of the oncoming car becomes larger, the rate at which it becomes larger is roughly computed automatically, again by our brain. With experience one will develop some judgment in that regard. Until that judgment has developed, it is important to be safe rather than sorry, i. e. to be extra cautious and to be certain that you are safely turning and not turning directly into the path of an oncoming car. On a four lane road, you might be aware of the oncoming cars in the center lane, but you could miss an oncoming car in the right lane because the car in the center lane creates an angle (like a shadow) that can obscure a car in the right lane.

When you are turning, you also have to be certain that no pedestrians or bicyclists or other obstructions are crossing in the crosswalk that traverses the street into which you are about to turn, since you may have to suddenly brake for a pedestrian, which will cause you to be stuck directly in the path of an oncoming car. Remember to be cautious since there are "no do-overs."

> **If you are in the middle of an intersection, waiting to turn left, and there is an opposing car also waiting to turn left, that opposing car may be blocking your view of a car in the lane adjacent to the opposing car. Leaning far to your left may give you a better view, otherwise best to be patient and wait for an unobstructed view.**

Putting the shoe on the other foot, if you are a car that is approaching a traffic light at an intersection, and you see that there is an opposing car waiting to turn left, you have to be very certain that the car is not going to turn in front of you, either because their light has changed and yours hasn't, or because they have misjudged your speed, or even that they haven't seen you. This is another reason for driving at the proper speed so that you can safely brake if the light turns to yellow, or the opposing car turns in front of you. There are some intersections that will say "No Left Turn" and sometimes there will be certain hours when left turns are prohibited.

There are some intersections where left turns may be particularly difficult because of the time of day, or they have a traffic pattern that rarely presents a safe opening. There may also be a long line waiting for a left turn arrow or other opportunity to turn left. It is often a wise decision to go past that intersection and to turn right at the next corner and then to turn right twice again so that in effect you have made a left turn. If you know the area well, you can also turn left a block after passing the difficult left turn intersection, and then make another left turn and then a right turn so that you would have gone one or two less blocks than had you made three right turns. One way streets may alter this.

Coming out of a side street or an alley or driveway, there may be cross traffic going both ways, and sometimes the timing is such that there will seldom be an opening. Occasionally you will ultimately decide to make a right turn when you have a safe opening and then get into the left lane and turn left and make two more left turns and then a right turn to get back onto the street that you were originally going to turn left onto. Instead of turning left three times, you might, after turning left, be able to turn into a driveway or alley and then to carefully back up and turn around, and come back to the street that you were trying to turn left onto.

When turning left into a busy street, or even crossing an intersection, don't assume that a car coming from your right is going to go across the intersection since that car might in fact be turning left in front of you even without signaling. If you are the car that is turning in front of a car that is waiting to cross the intersection and/or turning left, be aware that they might think you are going straight. Be sure your turn signal is on and be sure that they are not pulling out in front of you.

It is important to signal at least 100 feet before an intersection if you are intending to turn in either direction, and you could signal even earlier. However, *if there is an intersection or parking lot entrance or exit before the intersection that you want to turn left or right into, try not to signal the turn until you have passed that first intersection or exit (or entrance) because you might mislead other drivers at that first intersection, or parking lot exit, entrance or driveway.*

Don't turn and go over the safety island or marking to get into a left turn lane before the markers indicate that it is proper, because a car in front of you might be waiting to turn legally and properly into the left turn lane, and they might legally suddenly turn left into you, as you illegally pass them. If you are **legally** changing into a left turn lane, always be certain that there are no cars **illegally** passing you on your left.

Whatever you are intending to do at a stop sign, if the car on your left or right is a van, truck or SUV, you may not be able to see the traffic coming from your right or left side until the larger and/or higher vehicle has gone through the intersection, in order to clear your view. You will simply have to wait. Sometimes, moving forward a foot or two (legally), may give you the visibility you safely need, and sometimes just not pulling up quite so far to begin with, you might maintain some visibility. *Remember that when stopping for a stop sign, only one car at a time can legally proceed when safe to do so.*

If you are turning left and there is a car about to turn left going in the same direction as you, but in front of you, you may not be able to see a car that is coming from the opposite direction, until the car in front of you has turned. This is particularly true of a van or high SUV or truck.

Always stay to the right of the divider or marker, and this is always important, especially at night, to avoid ever going the wrong way, which can be very dangerous and often fatal.

Turning left into a divided or four lane highway, you should turn into the center lane of the road that you have turned into. If you are turning left where two lanes are marked to turn left, be certain that you turn into the left lane and if you are in the right lane of those two lanes turning left, make sure you end up in the right lane into which you were turning. Be aware of arrows painted on the road to indicate three possible directions you can go, either straight, turning left, or turning right (or combinations), i.e. the arrow may indicate straight and/or right and/or left turn.

While waiting to turn left at an intersection, keep your wheels straight so that you are less likely to be pushed into the path of an oncoming car, if you are struck from behind.

SUMMARY: When turning left at an intersection, be especially aware that the oncoming cars may have a different timing of their lights, so don't assume anything. Be very cautious and patient until you have developed experience either as the car turning left, or the car intending to go straight approaching an intersection where an oncoming car is waiting to turn left. Be aware of pedestrians or bicyclists or other obstructions that may be in the path of your turn. Don't go over a safety island to get into a left turn lane before the markings indicate that it is allowed, and if your car is waiting to turn legally and properly into the left turn lane, watch for a car that might be improperly on your left.

ALCOHOL AND OTHER DRUGS AND MEDICATIONS WHICH CAN AFFECT DRIVING

I N ILLINOIS, AND ALL OTHER STATES, a blood alcohol concentration (BAC) of 0.08% or higher is considered Driving Under the Influence (DUI), but any level of alcohol can seriously affect driving ability and safety.

> **Teenagers beginning to drive, or even mature drivers should be encouraged and required to have a "designated driver" who has not been drinking alcohol or using any other substance which could affect driving, including marijuana.**

For detailed information on graduated licensing laws as well as regulations regarding DUI's, the reader is referred to their state driver's manual. This can change from year to year. There may be an alternative to suspension of driving privileges for first time DUI offenders who wish to obtain driving relief during their statutory suspension period, by agreeing to a breathalyzer test before each subsequent driving (ignition interlock), involving significant financial outlay.

In Illinois it is illegal for anyone to drink alcoholic beverages in the vehicle. It is illegal to have alcohol in the passenger area of the vehicle if the container has been opened. If you are under age 21, and are stopped and issued a citation for a traffic violation and found to have any trace of alcohol in your system while operating a motor vehicle, your driving privileges will be suspended for three months. **Remember "Friends Don't Let Friends Drive Drunk."**

SUMMARY: In Illinois and probably in most other states, it is illegal for anyone to drink alcoholic beverages in the vehicle. It is illegal to have alcohol in the passenger area of the vehicle if the container has been opened. If you are under age 21, and are stopped and issued a citation for a traffic violation, and found to have any trace of alcohol in your system while operating a motor vehicle, your driving privileges will be suspended for three months. At any age, it is far better not to drive when you've had anything alcoholic to drink, or any medication or drug which could impair judgment, reflexes, and perception.

DROWSINESS OR TIREDNESS

> Never drive when you are drowsy. Pull off the road and get some sleep or exercise, get fresh air, take a break. Don't try to fight through it. Even a short nap can make you much more alert. Stop in a safe place, not on the road or shoulder, lock the doors and take a nap.

ALCOHOL CAN INCREASE DROWSINESS. THIS IS especially true in late adolescence and young adults. Get enough sleep every night. If you have obstructive sleep apnea or insomnia or any other type of sleep disorder, obtain medical help from a doctor who specializes in sleep medicine. Reaction time is slower and awareness is decreased and judgment is impaired in drivers who are tired. **If you are traveling long distances, stop at least every two hours, or every 100 miles, pull into a rest area, and take a fifteen or twenty minute break.**

Your chances of being involved in a crash are obviously much greater if you are driving and falling asleep, in contrast to your chances if you were alert. Many new-driver crashes involve drivers who were drowsy. Cars with a drowsy or sleeping driver often drift out of their lane until they hit something, and they usually show no signs of braking. "Drowsy driving crashes" often occur late at night or early in the morning, often involving a single vehicle which leaves the roadway. The driver is often alone in the vehicle. Contrary to most belief, teens need more sleep than adults, due to brain and hormonal changes. Unfortunately, they often get much less, between homework, activities, delayed sleep rhythms, and school days that start early. It is often the so-called good kids, even the high achievers who seem to have more sleep related accidents. Some cars now offer lane drifting alert as an option, however with snow, ice and any other severe weather conditions, the lane markings may not be apparent. Look for improvements in this safety feature possibly related to GPS. Although Caffeine can block the sleep receptors in the brain temporarily, it is better to pull into a safe spot and take a nap for 20 minutes. Ideally have another awake adult with you who can speak to you. Switching the driving to a rested passenger may be another option, but switch in a safe location.

As a recently retired allergist, I am aware that allergy itself can cause extreme drowsiness, whether it be from unsuspected or even known food and/or inhalant allergy.

> **Do NOT use cruise control if you are even slightly tired. If you fall asleep, your car will continue at the set speed until hitting another car, tree, pole, ditch, water, or another object or hazard.**

Drivers who work late shifts, particularly if they work rotating late shifts, might be especially apt to drive when tired, fatigued, or drowsy. Medical residents who are on call for extended periods often have a higher incidence of accidents driving home after their shift.

> **SUMMARY: Don't drive if drowsy or tired. Pull off the road and get some sleep or exercise, get fresh air, take a break and don't try to fight through it. Even a short nap can make you more alert, but do stop in a safe place. Lock the doors and take a nap. The hours late in the night or early in the morning are particularly troublesome. Don't use cruise control if you are even slightly tired.**

STEERING

IT IS IMPORTANT TO HOLD THE steering wheel preferably at 9:00 and 3:00 o'clock. Some steering wheels are built so that you can't grip them in those locations, and in that case, then 10:00 and 2:00 would be preferable, and some instructors suggest 8:00 and 4:00. In this position, an accident causing the air bags to inflate will less likely drive your arms into your face, possibly causing injury to both your arms and your face.

While many instructors will teach students to not move either hand beyond 12:00 or 6:00 in order to keep the hands, during turning, out of the path of an inflating airbag, my own thought is that if you are used to using hand over hand type turning which many of us learned years ago, it is better to concentrate on safely turning, no matter which technique you are comfortable with. If you are thinking about the newer teaching, which does make some sense, and you are distracted enough that you get into an accident, then you've won the battle but lost the war. Do what is comfortable and keep your eyes and your thoughts on the road.

Drivers need to keep both hands on the steering wheel. Smoking in the car, whether driving or as a passenger, is a bad idea. It is better to keep your arms inside the car, and your hands on the steering wheel. Don't use hand gestures as part of conversation while driving.

The minimum distance from the steering wheel should be 10 inches (preferably 12) to protect yourself or lessen the chance of injury due to inflation of air bags. The driver's side airbag should be aimed at your chest and not your neck, face, or head.

A driver should not turn their head to look at passengers with whom they are conversing, but rather look ahead, and scan the mirrors.

Many instructors teach putting the thumb up alongside the steering wheel rather than wrapping it underneath, feeling that this will prevent undue injury to the thumbs from inflation of an airbag. While I respect these authorities, I have not been able to convince myself that wrapping the thumb underneath would in fact increase injuries, because if the hands are in the right place, the airbag should not really impinge upon them. If the hands are at 12:00 or 6:00 o'clock or near there, then I can understand why that might come into play. If you are more comfortable, as I am, with your thumb underneath and wrapped around the steering wheel, then I think that's the way you should drive. I'm open to corrections and suggestions from readers as well as any other sources.

> **SUMMARY:** It is important to hold the steering wheel at 9:00 and 3:00 o'clock, or if necessary, 10:00 and 2:00 o'clock. It is also important that the steering wheel should be at least 10 inches, or preferably 12 inches from the driver to lessen the chance of injury due to inflation of airbags, which should be aimed at your chest and not your neck, face, or head. The driver should not turn their head to look at passengers to converse, but rather look ahead, and scan the mirrors. Keep both hands on the wheel.

BRAKING

Anti-lock Braking Systems (ABS) generally kick in during heavy braking applications, but sometimes even lighter braking on slippery roads may cause them to activate. Basically they pump the brakes using a computer and the advantage is sometimes a shorter stopping distance on slippery roads, and probably more predictably, the maintenance of steering control. With ABS you will feel the jerking through the brake pedal and you will most likely hear it as well. **Don't let up, but keep pressing down because the computer is doing the intermittent brake pumping for you.** The purpose of this is to avoid a locked up wheel, which will slide, and prevent you from effective steering. If your car does not have an anti-lock braking system, then pumping the brakes, just short of locking up the wheels, will help both steering and stopping. If you are not sure whether or not your car has this feature, on a slippery surface, with nothing around you, put the brake on fairly hard and if you hear and feel the pumping action then you will know that you have ABS. It is usually indicated as an icon on the dash and would be noted as a safety feature on a new car window sticker. Most, if not all, newer cars do have this safety feature.

If you think your brakes might be failing, pump them gently, and that will usually restore them. If your brakes give out on a level area, and there are cars in front of you, honk your horn, put your flashers on, steer around the cars if necessary, and use your emergency (parking) brake. If possible, shift into a lower gear in a stepwise manner (although this could damage the gears at higher speeds), it might help to slow and eventually stop the car.

If your brakes give out and you are going downhill, or you are on a mountain, you may be better off trying to put the emergency (parking) brake on, shifting the car into a lower and even the lowest gear. If you are not going too fast, you may decide to run off the road into the side which could be a fence or guard rail or trees, or into the mountain itself. In trying to hit an obstacle in order to slow or stop, a glancing blow is usually safer than a head on contact. You may have to do this even on a level road. It is important to remember not to hit a guardrail at the end terminal, i.e. the beginning as you might approach it, marked with diagonal black stripes alternating with yellow stripes, and this is because of a possible slight change in the width of some guardrails which could cause part of the guardrail to sheer off and even pierce the car and seriously injure the driver.

> If you have driven through standing water, test your brakes by gently pumping them. If they are wet, usually pumping them up to six to ten times will usually dry them and restore their braking ability.

> SUMMARY: Make sure you know if you have anti-lock brakes, because if you do, you just keep pushing harder on the brake and it will intermittently cut in and out to help keep the wheels from locking up. If your brakes give out on a level area, you might be able, honking your horn and putting on your emergency flashers, to steer around cars if necessary, and use your emergency (parking) brake. You should also shift into a lower gear. Put your signal on, take your foot off the gas pedal and coast to a stop on the side of the road or the shoulder. This approach would be especially appropriate if there were few cars close behind you, particularly if it is not a high speed road. If your brakes give out and you are going downhill, especially on a mountain, besides putting your emergency (parking) brake on, and shifting the car into a lower and even the lowest gear, consider running off the road into the side which could be a fence or guardrail, or trees, with a glancing blow, or into the mountain itself. You may even have to do this on a level road.

DISTRACTIONS INSIDE THE CAR

"Driving Is A Full Time Job"

D ISTRACTIONS ARE NOT LISTED IN ORDER of importance, but using a cell phone and especially texting, even if both are hands free, is a very significant and often deadly distraction. Not all of these will apply to every driver, and each driver will need to prioritize the likelihood of each distraction affecting them.

Distractions can include the following:

- **Talk or conversation, especially with multiple passengers**
- **Talking on a cell phone, even a hands-free cell phone, (while this may be somewhat less distracting since it doesn't require as much use of the hands, recent studies have suggested there is actually as much distraction as there is with hand-held cellular phones). If you have to talk on a cellular phone, either hand held or hands free, pull over to a safe spot off the road or pull into a parking lot or side street to carry on the conversation. It is advised to not answer if driving, and when in a safe location, pick up voice mails, and return calls if necessary. In Illinois and other states, talking on a hand held cell phone is illegal, except in certain emergency situations.**
- **Texting on a cell phone is particularly bad, since it not only takes away one or two hands, but usually also visual contact from driving. This is said to increase the chance of an accident by many fold. Unfortunately, there have been many innocent victims who have been fatally injured because of crashes which have occurred because drivers were texting. In some studies it**

has been suggested that it may take 15 to 30 seconds to refocus on your driving after even voice activated texting in a car.

- Smoking. This is not a good idea while driving, for a number of reasons.
- Drivers have choked on food or drink, and hot liquids can potentially be harmful, even in a minor accident, or even with a sudden stop or swerve, unless the food container is tightly capped. Avoid eating and/or drinking while driving.
- Shaving
- Putting on make up
- Combing or brushing one's hair
- Listening to an MP3 player or any other electronic device with or without ear phones
- "Messing" with the knobs on the dash which could include the following;
  - Global Positioning Satellite (GPS), programming should be done before you start out or when you are stopped at a stop light, or in a parking lot. Changing or resetting of the GPS, using Smartphones or any electronic or computer controlled device can sometimes be delegated to a passenger.
  - Radio
  - Air conditioning
  - Heater
  - Defroster and rear defogger
- Any other electronic or other device that your car may be equipped with; some recent surveys of drivers have indicated that touch screens may be more distracting than control knobs.
- Adjusting or looking too long at mirrors
- Reading, including reading maps
- Writing
- Working on a computer
- Infants or small children in the back seat who are hungry or crying, or raising a fuss in any manner; pull over to a safe place and stop in order to more safely handle the situation.
- Pets that are not restrained or adequately secured
- Cleaning eyeglasses

- Changing eyeglasses, i.e. putting on sunglasses or taking off sunglasses, or putting on reading, distance, or multi-focal glasses; if you have new bifocals, or even a new prescription, be sure you are used to the adjustment before driving, especially in heavy traffic or on high speed roads.
- Reaching for a facial tissue
- Violent Sneezing or Coughing lasting more than a second or two
- Putting something in or removing an item from, the glove compartment or console compartment
- Hugging or kissing (or other expressions of affection)
- A stinging, flying, crawling or biting insect or other pest that has gained access to the inside of the car
- Reaching into a purse or similar accessory for any reason, while the vehicle is moving
- Loose balloons (They should be in the trunk, or in a large bag, or tied somewhere where they won't obstruct the drivers view.)
- Any object or objects including the results of shopping, either grocery or otherwise, piled or stacked up so high so as to block the view from the rear view mirror, and even pose a danger of loose flying objects in a sudden stop, turn or crash; items, in general, are best put on the back seat floor, or even more safely, in the trunk.

These distractions are applicable only to moving cars. It has been suggested that a 20 year old person chatting on a cell phone has responses equal to a 70 year old driver. There can be a marked variability of concentration abilities in either age group.

Hands-free cellular phones such as Blue Tooth set-ups, even with hands free dialing, may require you to push buttons on the steering wheel to initiate, or to answer a call, and that can be distracting.

It's illegal in many cities and even entire states to make or even take a cellular phone call while you are driving, particularly if it is not hands free. In many areas, any use of a cell phone, even hands free, such as in school and construction zones, is illegal and may result in a substantial fine.

If, while driving, you do have to initiate a **_LEGAL_** hands-free call on a cell phone or mobile phone that requires pushing buttons on the steering wheel, do it only when you are going in a straight direction and only if you have a system that operates with a minimum of distraction. Maintain a safe interval behind the car in front of you.

Request a passenger, if available, in the front seat to adjust air conditioning, heating or radio, or any other electronic or mechanical functions in the car. If you have a GPS, set it before driving and if it has to be reset, do it in a safe spot or have a passenger do it. If a phone call has to be made, ask the passenger to handle it.

REMEMBER, DRIVING IS A FULL TIME JOB. FOCUS ON GETTING YOURSELF AND YOUR PASSENGERS TO YOUR DESTINATION SAFELY.

SUMMARY: Multiple distractions can be encountered but especially any type of cell phone use, particularly texting, should be avoided. Driving is a full time job and the focus should be on that and not on anything else. Passengers can often assist the driver in certain functions such as GPS setting, handling phone calls, or operating air conditioning or heating and similar functions. You should not be multi-tasking while driving.

DISTRACTIONS OUTSIDE OF THE CAR

D ISTRACTIONS OUTSIDE OF THE CAR CAN be any of the following:

- A pedestrian crossing or about to cross your path, or walking on either side of the road
- An emergency vehicle
- An accident by the side of the road or in front of you, or even behind you or on either side
- A "badly speeding car" approaching from any direction
- A charity solicitor at a corner when the traffic light is green
- An unusual car, bus, truck or building or an unusually attractive scene, such as a vista from a mountain drive, rock formations, canyons, bodies of water, and beaches
- Unusual, or at times threatening, cloud formations
- **A car or especially a truck tailgating you**
- A sky writer or a low flying airplane, helicopter, blimp, or perhaps even a low flying drone
- An unusual, interesting or eye-catching and distinctive person; sometimes a person dressed in a costume and/or holding a sign soliciting or advertising business for a nearby establishment such as a car wash, or a newly opened restaurant
- Extremely heavy traffic
- Bad weather; either rain, snow, ice, wind, or fog
- Unusual dogs or other pets that are being walked (or running loose)
- Animals such as squirrels, birds, or larger animals, either on the road, or at the side or edge of the road, or grazing

- Interesting and attractive floral arrangements in yards, and trees, especially flowering in the Spring, or changing colors in the Fall
- Houses or other buildings under construction, or for sale
- A fence, a new fence, or a change in a fence
- A full moon or an unusually large moon
- Unusual or interesting cars or trucks parked or on the road
- Too many roadside signs, whether advertising or highway department signs.

I have witnessed drivers noticing and commenting on all of the above potential distractions outside the car.

As with distractions inside the car, I'm sure that readers will recall some of their own unique distractions.

SUMMARY: Distractions outside of the car can include other vehicles, persons, buildings, nature driven scenes, animals, pets, floral arrangements, and astronomical items. This is only a partial list. The emphasis should be on focusing on driving.

SEATBELTS, AIRBAGS AND CHILD SAFETY SEATS USING L.A.T.C.H

Seatbelts and Child Safety Seats using L.A.T.C.H.

THE SHOULDER BELT SHOULD COME ACROSS the chest, halfway between the shoulder and the neck, in other words, in the middle of the collar bone. Too close to the shoulder, the belt can slip off, and too close to the neck, it could cause serious injury. The lap belt should come snugly across the upper part of the thighs, and should not come across the abdomen.

Seat belts have clearly saved many lives over the last 30 or 40 years. They have become better as advances are made. Some cars have pre-tensioners which mean that the driver and passenger can be relatively comfortable, but with impact the belts tighten up quickly. There are also shoulder belts that can inflate in an accident, available in some cars.

Although technically not pertaining to seatbelts, it is important to have head rests properly adjusted. Ideally the top of the head rest should be even with the top of the head, or extend slightly above it.

It is extremely important to always buckle up and it is against the law in most states to not do this. It is also extremely important that passengers in the backseat, as well as the front seat, buckle up. Simply stated, it is important for *EVERY* person in the car to be buckled up before the car moves.

Avoid having rubber bands, paper clips, even facial tissue or any other small items that could accidentally get stuck in the seatbelt buckle latch, preventing connection.

Pregnant women should also use shoulder and lap seatbelts in the prescribed fashion.

L.A.T.C.H. stands for Lower Anchors and Tethers for Children. This is a way of installing a child safety seat without having to use vehicle seatbelts. L.A.T.C.H. child safety seats have either flexible or rigid anchors that attach to rigid anchors in the vehicle. The vehicle anchors are situated at the junction of the vehicle's seat back and bottom. The top tethers are only used when these safety seats are used facing forward. A rear facing infant seat should never be placed in a vehicle equipped with an airbag at that location.

Some booster seats also have L.A.T.C.H. so that the booster doesn't move around on the vehicle seat. Some vehicles will allow L.A.T.C.H. installation in a middle seating position. Check your owner's manual. L.A.T.C.H. including tethers are only used until a child reaches a 45 lb. limit, although you should check your vehicle owner's manual and car seat for instructions in that regard. Installation of a L.A.T.C.H. child safety seat should be checked by a child/infant seat installation specialist, and you can check with your local police station, AAA or a driving school to get locations, or go to "SafeSeats4Kids" on the Internet (see page 159).

Airbags

Some advanced frontal airbags have sensors which consider factors such as the occupants size, the seat position, whether the seatbelt is buckled, if there are pre-tensioners, and the crash severity, to determine the speed at which the driver and the front passenger airbags will inflate. Unfortunately drivers and passengers who were too close to airbags, especially if they were small framed or frail, have been injured and even killed because of deploying airbags. Airbags can sometimes deploy without a crash, and sometimes they can fail to deploy. In 2014 and 2015 there were extensive recalls of millions of cars because of airbags made by Takata. Not all of these have been replaced and in some instances the replacements were also defective. These bags would explode with such pressure that metallic shards acting as shrapnel would be discharged, injuring and even killing drivers and passengers.

If you purchase a used car, you should be certain, if it was in a crash, that the airbags have been replaced, and you should be certain that these are not defective airbags. Carfax may be a way to check into that. Cars cleaned up after being involved in flooding may not necessarily appear on a Carfax report. Refer to more information on the airbag recall in the potpourri section and additional reminders toward the back of *Sane Driving in a Mad World*.

If you wear glasses you might wish to obtain Polycarbonate driving glasses or sunglasses, which could even fit over regular prescription glasses in an attempt to prevent airbag injury to the eyes. It is a good idea to check with an eye specialist to be sure that whatever you are wearing is likely to be protective and not cause more harm.

Although the original airbags were designed to be used only for frontal impact and protect the driver and the passenger in the front seat, additional airbags have been added and side impact air bags are available that will deploy if there is an impact from the side. Side curtain airbags are also known as head curtain airbags and generally span the length of the cabin and provide head protection, particularly in the case of a roll over. Side curtain airbags stay inflated for a few seconds to block the side windows and prevent the occupants from being ejected. Although it is often recommended that children not lean up against side airbags, there apparently thus far have not been any serious injuries to children as a result of inflation.

Recent safety criteria essentially requires the presence of some form of side impact airbags, since safety testing is virtually impossible to do acceptably without having side airbag head protection.

Airbags are supplemental restraint systems (SABS), and must be used with seatbelts, otherwise protection is greatly diminished.

It is also cautioned to *never* place a rear facing infant seat in a vehicle equipped with an air bag at that location.

The safest place for a child or an adult passenger to be seated in a car with side airbags, and in fact with or without them, is in the middle seat of the back row if there is one.

In spite of some personal difficulty that I had with spontaneously deploying airbags, I would recommend the use of unaffected (not defective) airbags routinely, and I continue to keep them activated in my present car, as opposed to the car where they deployed spontaneously, which I drove for a number of years with them turned off. It is very important to make sure there is no recall and to address it if there is. If you have a car with front seats only and no rear seat, and a child has to be transported frequently, you can apply to NHTSA for permission to request cut-off or on/off switches to the passenger airbag. It is important to keep in touch with the manufacturer and dealer and also NHTSA and safercars.gov to try to be aware when there are recalls.

SUMMARY: All passengers in all seats should have their seatbelts buckled before the car moves. There have been failures on the part of airbags and recently extensive recalls of airbags made by Takata. Since explosion, particularly in hot, humid climates can occur, with shrapnel injuring or even killing drivers or passengers, it is important to get this corrected or find an alternative. Airbags must be used with seatbelts in order to provide maximum protection. A rear facing infant seat should never be placed in a vehicle equipped with an airbag at that location.

ENTERING AND EXITING YOUR CAR

WHEN ENTERING YOUR CAR IT SHOULD be from the curb side if this is possible. Very few cars these days have bench seats and it can be very difficult to scoot over to the driver's side when there is a center console and/or bucket seats. Entering from the street side, you should stand on the curbing and observe traffic, **and only enter when there is sufficient time for you to open the door, get in, and close the door, since otherwise you may force a passing car into an adjacent lane, or cause them to stop suddenly to avoid striking you.** The time it takes can depend upon the type of key you have, whether you have a remote control car door opener, how fresh the remote battery is, how agile you are, and possibly other circumstances, such as ice and snow, or rain and umbrellas. Passengers in the rear seat should ideally enter from the curb side when there is moving traffic on the driver's side.

Exiting a car is also especially an area where you need to be aware that an open car door can cause a passing motorist or bicyclist to swerve to avoid striking you. You should check your rear view and side view mirror, and look out the side windows to be certain that there is no approaching traffic before you attempt to exit. You need to develop some sense as to how far away cars should be before you attempt to safely exit (or enter) your car and approximately how long it will take you to do either under various circumstances.

SUMMARY: Whether entering or exiting a car it is important, especially if entering or exiting from the driver's side, to be sure that there is sufficient time for you to open and close the door, get in or out, close the door, and safely leave the traffic side of the car otherwise you may force a passing car into an adjacent lane, or cause them to stop suddenly to avoid striking the door or you. How agile you are, the type of key you have, and the weather conditions all enter into an intelligent decision as to whether or not you have time to safely enter or exit a car. Be aware that an open car door can cause a passing motorist, bicyclist, or motorcyclist to swerve to avoid striking the door or you.

TRAFFIC LIGHTS

B E AWARE THAT WHEN THERE IS an electrical failure involving traffic lights, or traffic lights are malfunctioning for whatever reason, usually the red stop light is either flashing, or there is a stop sign at the intersection. If the lights are completely out, that's actually the most dangerous situation. Any of these scenarios means that the intersection becomes a three or four way stop, depending upon how many streets intersect. If two or more drivers arrive and stop at the same time, it is the driver on the right who generally goes first, but never insist on the right-of-way.

Red light cameras (photo enforced) at intersections are a mixed blessing. Drivers have complained about these intersections, since they tend to stop suddenly for fear of getting a ticket, and they are concerned about being hit from behind. If you are going slowly enough so that you can safely stop, as you should be, then that's what you should do. Many critics have suggested that the cameras are simply a means of obtaining additional income for the governmental bodies responsible for installing them. While that might be true sometimes, there have been instances where they have reduced the rate of serious crashes at certain intersections, and other instances where it has actually increased. There has been an increase in rear end collisions at many of these photo enforced intersections. One complaint that I share with others is that some municipalities have shortened the duration of the yellow caution light, thereby increasing the number of automatic tickets issued, increasing the financial productivity, albeit unfairly.

> **At any traffic light intersection, especially if you are the lead car, when the light changes to green, always hesitate for a second or two, and look to make sure that cars that are coming in the cross traffic are stopping or have stopped. *Watch for emergency vehicles also.* This slight hesitation can be life saving.**

Most drivers, with experience, will pretty much know at what point they are going to go through a yellow light, i.e. they really can't safely stop, as they are approaching the intersection. Factors affecting this are; if there is an opposing car waiting to turn left in front of you, are you driving at a legal or safe speed, and the third factor, which shouldn't really be a factor, is if someone is seriously tailgating you and there is no car in oncoming traffic that is turning in front of you. It then becomes a matter of judgment. I would emphasize that if a car is seriously tailgating you, you should still be going slowly enough that you could safely stop, and the car behind you should be able to stop as well. This is again where judgment and experience play an important role.

If you are familiar with the intersection, you may be aware of how long the light stays green before it changes to caution, and you also may be aware that some caution lights are for only several seconds, and some are longer.

LEFT TURN ON ARROW

THERE ARE TWO KINDS OF LEFT turn signals, i.e. arrows. One is where a sign states "Left Turn on Arrow Only." Then there is a second situation where there is a left turn arrow, and you can turn left on the arrow, but you can also turn left when the arrow goes off, as long as your light is green. This assumes that there is no immediately oncoming traffic, and again if there is no sign that says, "Left Turn on Arrow Only," and there is **no red left turn arrow light on**. In other words, you can go into the intersection with a green light, and you can wait until traffic has cleared and then turn left, rather than waiting in the left turn lane for the left turn arrow in the next traffic light cycle.

While waiting for a green left turn arrow, be alert and pay attention so that you don't hold up the cars behind you. Try not to be asleep at the wheel, but make sure that when you start your left turn, that the cars coming toward you from the opposite direction have not started up, accidentally misreading their signal. As usual, be sure that the intersection has been cleared of cross traffic, especially cars turning left from your right, in the cross traffic.

> **If you are the lead car in a left turn arrow lane, make sure that you have pulled up close enough to the intersection to trigger the arrow.**

When you are turning left, especially on a left turn arrow, keep a safe distance from the car in front of you. According to your skill and experience, try not to make it an excessive distance in order that you enable the greatest possible number of cars to safely get through while the arrow is still on.

If you are in the left turn lane and all of a sudden you decide that you don't want to turn left, be totally certain that there is no traffic in the lane or lanes that you are going to pull into to go straight or turn right. You would be making a last minute decision which can always have the potential for danger. If there is any question, stay where you are and make the turn and get back to where you want to be, going another way. **Do not put other drivers in jeopardy by last minute sudden and erratic decisions.**

It is important to avoid the bad, rude, unsafe, and perhaps simply distracted or incompetent drivers. If you see such blatantly bad behavior, try to get their license number and car description and phone it into the police department if you are in a position to safely do that. In many areas * 999 will transmit the information to the proper local officials. If there is undue delay in reaching * 999 or if you sense great danger from a very badly driven car, then you can dial the police directly. Generally, I would reserve 9-1-1 for a life threatening emergency. A seriously unsafe driver may be just that (life threatening). Be prepared to be identified as the caller, to discourage fraudulent calls. If you have a passenger who could make the call, that's better and less distracting for you. In some locations, if you cannot reach 9-1-1, try 1-1-2, again for emergency calls only.

When you are turning left on an arrow, watch for the opposing traffic that might turn right, into your path, even if there are "no turn on right" signs posted. If there are two lanes to turn into, theoretically you are turning into the left lane and that driver is turning into the right lane. While that may not always be illegal unless there is "No Turn on Red," it is still distracting and disruptive when that driver turns right. Drivers are advised not to turn right when there is an arrow allowing opposing drivers to turn left, unless there is an obvious safe opening, usually in an extremely wide intersection with three or more lanes in each direction. Be certain that oncoming traffic does not have a longer green light or a longer arrow, so that you know that when your light changes, that doesn't necessarily mean that their light is changing.

Right Turn On Red

We have all seen frequent violations regarding right turn on red when the driver doesn't stop, or even slow down, but just rolls through a red light to turn right, especially often trying to beat the cross traffic cars that are starting up with a green light.

Always watch for pedestrians and always give them the right of way whether they are crossing in front of you or illegally crossing the street into which you are about to turn. **Come to a complete stop before you turn,** although some photo enforced intersections will not create a ticket if you **slowly** roll through the red light, i.e. turning right without coming to a complete stop. Check your local ordinances.

"No Right Turn On Red"

It is very important to notice the "No Right Turn On Red" signs. Some of these signs will give certain hours where this is prohibited and some will simply state "No Right Turn On Red," in which case you must wait until the light changes to make your turn. Some will say, "No Right Turn On Red if Pedestrians are Present."

If there is a sign that says "No Right Turn On Red," but there is a green arrow for a right turn permitting it, then that supersedes the sign and you can make a right turn, but always be watchful for a car that might still be in the intersection. If there is a sign that says "No Turn on Red" but there is a green arrow for a left turn, the green arrow, supersedes the sign, but as always, be watchful.

When turning in either direction, always watch out for pedestrians, bicyclists, motorcyclists, skateboarders, and anyone or anything else that could be in your path.

SUMMARY: At any traffic light intersection, if you are lead car, when the light changes to green, always hesitate for a second or two, and look to make sure that cars that are coming in the cross traffic are stopping or have stopped. Be alert for emergency vehicles. If you are being seriously tailgated by another car, you should still be going slowly enough that you can safely stop, and the car behind you should be able to stop as well. When there is a sign that states "Left Turn on Arrow Only," that means exactly what it says. If there is a left turn arrow, but no sign that states "Left Turn on Arrow Only," you can turn left when the arrow goes off, as long as your light is green, and there is no immediately oncoming traffic. In this situation ordinarily there will *not* be a red left turn arrow light on. On "Left Turn on Arrow Only" situations, be alert so that you don't hold up the cars behind you. Always be sure that the intersection has been cleared of cross traffic, especially cars turning left from the cross traffic on your right. Try to keep a safe, but not excessive distance, between the car in front of you on turning on the arrow so that you enable as many cars as possible to turn left while the arrow is on. With right turn on red, always watch for and give the right of way to pedestrians. Come to a complete stop before you turn. With "No Right Turn on Red," there may be certain hours, or the presence of pedestrians, which may prohibit the right turn on red. If there is a sign that says "No Right Turn on Red" but there is a green arrow for a right turn permitting it, that supersedes the sign and you can make a right turn, but always be watchful for a car that might still be in the intersection. A left turn green arrow supersedes a sign stating "No Turn on Red."

ENTERING AND DRIVING ON THE ROADWAY

WHEN PULLING OUT OF A PARKING lot, driveway, alley, or side street, stop at the white line, and if no white line, stop at the sidewalk, and if there is no sidewalk, stop at the street (curb) before you enter it.

Don't stick out into traffic where other cars may have to go around you when you are entering a street from an alleyway or a parking lot, or entering a road from a side street. That creates a dangerous situation causing cars to swerve around you, or to stop. Even just pulling up too quickly to that point can cause a driver to swerve into another lane and possibly into another car. If a car has stopped because of a car sticking out into the street, if you are in the center lane of a four lane road, you should also stop to allow the impatient and possibly incompetent, careless, or inconsiderate driver to enter or cross the roadway or turn left. The car wishing to turn left may not have actually been sticking out, and the car stopping may just be a courteous driver who is allowing another driver to enter or cross the lane, rather than blocking the driver's attempt to enter or turn. Alertness will enable you to cooperate in that display of courtesy.

> **If you are the car that is stopping, be aware of fast moving cars in the adjacent or oncoming lanes that may not be able to stop. SOMETIMES BEING COURTEOUS CAN ACTUALLY CREATE A DANGEROUS SITUATION.**

When there are merging lanes, or accidents or construction causing lanes to merge, there or will often be drivers who think they are entitled, driving up close and expecting to be let in at the last minute near the head of the line. While some would advocate courtesy for the sake of expediency to the cars that are in the lane trying to merge, the proper thing for the driver who feels "entitled" would be to try to enter the open lane further back, demonstrating a sense of fairness and showing that he or she is not trying to feel entitled and not trying to outdo those who are obviously waiting their turn. There are a number of traffic engineers who suggest driving right up to the point of merging and asking both lanes to alternate. I disagree for a number of reasons, partly because this seems to be unfair, secondly because it could be another way to incite road rage. **Driving should not be a contest, but rather an opportunity for courtesy and cooperation.**

If you are a passenger in a car and the driver is driving this entitled way, within reason you have the right to point out to them that you are uncomfortable, and they shouldn't feel entitled, although you might very well choose to use other (your own) words. You might say, "You are special to me, but not necessarily to other drivers."

Narrow Residential Streets

Often on narrow residential streets, with cars parked on one or both sides, there isn't room for two cars to comfortably or safely pass going in opposite directions. Be courteous and pull into an open spot to allow the approaching car to pass, or if the approaching car has indicated that courtesy to you, then acknowledge that. Be aware that in the Fall, with leaves in the street, and with plowed snow also possibly narrowing the street, courtesy, caution and awareness are particularly important. If a snow plow has come through but had to go around illegally parked cars, there can be a little ledge of ice that forms that will also narrow the street and that ledge may be somewhat of an outline of the parked car the plow had to go around. Any icy ledge (car outline) sticking out into the street can be a serious obstacle for a car.

SUMMARY: When pulling out of a driveway, alley, or side street, stop at the sidewalk, and if there is no sidewalk, stop at the curb before entering the street. If you are stopping at an intersection or in the middle of a block because you see a child or pet crossing, or you are trying to be courteous to allow a car to enter, be sure that there is no fast moving car in the lane adjacent to you that may not be able to stop. Sometimes being courteous can actually create a potentially dangerous situation. With merging lanes, because of accidents or construction, try to be fair and not to pull up all the way to the point of entrance, but rather to try to merge somewhere back so that other drivers sense your intent to be fair. With narrow residential streets, possibly because of parked cars, mounds of snow, or leaves, if there is not room for both an oncoming car and your car, pull into an open spot to allow the oncoming car to safely pass you.

EXPRESSWAYS, ENTERING, DRIVING ON, AND EXITING

EXPRESSWAY DRIVING IS GENERALLY MORE DEMANDING **than other driving, and beginning drivers might reasonably delay this until they have had sufficient training and experience to be comfortable and safe.**

Not only are the speed limits higher, but unfortunately many of the cars on the expressway will be exceeding the speed limit. The beginning driver should pretty much stay in the right lane, although that poses a problem with encountering cars entering the expressway. As a driver develops confidence, they could then move over into the middle, and eventually into the left lane if necessary for passing purposes. If you are staying in the right lane, keep sufficient distance between you and the car in front of you to enable a merging car to safely enter the expressway.

The most common scenario of expressway entering is a merge approach lane, which, if fairly short, will make merging difficult, or if fairly long, will make merging easier. A merge approach lane for an expressway is intended to allow the car entering the expressway to build up speed equal to the cars traveling in the right lane of the expressway, so that, with an appropriate opening, the car can merge. *The driver should signal at the appropriate time that they are going to change from the merge approaching lane into the adjacent lane, but should first ascertain that there is in fact an opening.* Some driver education professionals suggest signaling before looking for the opening. I prefer ascertaining an opening before signaling.

A less common situation for entering an expressway would be a yield sign, and in this instance, the entering driver may need to slow down and even stop if necessary before finding a safe spot to enter the expressway. The yield situation is much more common as you leave an expressway and go onto a secondary road.

One pet peeve of mine is when drivers, particularly of large trucks, are going at high speed and not maintaining enough interval between them in the right lane to allow cars to safely merge onto the expressway.

Frequently, especially at periods of high traffic such as rush hours, there will be a control stop/go light on the ramp that is leading to the lane for the approach to enter the expressway. This functions to keep entering cars at a far enough distance apart to create less disruption to traffic.

Driving On Expressways

It is important to maintain a speed that is pretty much with the flow of traffic, however not to exceed the speed limit. That's sometimes an oxymoron because on many expressways, most of the cars are exceeding the speed limit. There are minimum speed limits, but cars traveling at the minimum speed limit generally create a hazard for other drivers. If you are not experienced enough to drive above the minimum speed, then probably you should delay traveling on the expressway until you are comfortable with the higher posted speed limits. The minimum speed more properly applies to cars that have developed mechanical problems after entering the expressway. When this happens, a driver should pull off the road or exit at the first safe opportunity so as not to impede traffic and possibly create a more dangerous situation. While driving slowly, they should also turn on their emergency flashers.

If cars are trying to pass you, carefully signal and move into another lane, usually to the right. Be aware of cars behind you by monitoring your rearview, and side view mirrors.

In terms of lane changing on expressways, it is important that there be no car in front of you which is stopping or slowing in the lane into which you are about to change. The less lane changing you do, the better. Lane changing is frequently the cause of accidents on expressways, and seldom saves enough time to make it worth the extra risk to the driver who frequently changes lanes, and to the other drivers who have to adjust to that type of aggressive driving.

Exiting Expressways

It is important to have some idea ahead of time as to when and where you need to exit an expressway to make sure you are in the correct lane to exit, before the actual exit. While this is most often the right lane, sometimes it will be the left lane, and usually signs will indicate the exit lane. It is a good idea to be familiar enough with the road so that you know the exit before *your* exit so that you have time to get over safely. If you are behind a large truck, you may miss the sign especially if you are unfamiliar with the area. You do need to signal and you need to slow down to the speed indicated on the sign as a safe exiting speed. This presumes that there is dry pavement. **With rain, snow, or ice, you may need to exit at a much slower speed so that you don't slide off the exit ramp.**

Often when exiting an expressway, there will be cars entering just before the exit ramp and you need to be aware of these entering vehicles and either slow down and let them go in front of you, or if the timing is such, you may be able to safely speed up to go in front of them. This again requires some judgment that comes with experience, and if there is any question, slowing down and allowing the entering car to go in front is often the safer choice. Always use your turn signals.

If you've already started to get off of an expressway and then realized that it was the wrong exit, it is almost always unsafe to try to get back on the expressway. If you are getting off of an expressway and you see that the exit is too crowded, and you are trying to get back on the expressway, it may be an understandable, but often an illegal and dangerous action, so if you do this at all, be extremely cautious. If you don't have a clearly safe path to abort your exit, just exit as you started to and then adjust to find your destination.

SUMMARY: It is suggested to drive at a speed that is pretty much with the flow of traffic, but not exceeding the speed limit. If you are not experienced enough to drive above the minimum speed, then probably you should delay traveling on the expressway until you are comfortable with the higher posted speed limits. The less lane changing you do, the better. It is a good idea to be familiar enough with the road so that you know the exit before your exit so that you have time to get over safely to the right lane or exit lane. Avoid being behind a large truck which may make it difficult for you to read the signs. With rain, snow, or ice, you may need to exit at a much slower speed so that you don't slide off the exit ramp. If you intend to abort your exit but don't have a clearly safe path, just exit as you started to, and then adjust to find your destination.

DRIVING IN LANES

WHILE DRIVING IN LANES IS ACTUALLY a different topic than changing lanes, obviously there is some overlap. Ordinarily you should only drive in the right lane, unless you are passing other cars. There will be some instances when you are approaching an exit and/or a merge enter situation where you might choose to move over to a left or center lane to avoid the merging and entering traffic. If there are three or more lanes going in the same direction, and if there are frequent entrances, some drivers will choose to stay in the center lane, i.e. the one between the left and the right lane, in order to avoid having to slow down every time there is an entrance of, or merging with, other cars. This is proper driving only if there will still be at least one or two open lanes to your left to allow faster cars to pass you if necessary. On a busy expressway, if you see drivers piling up behind you and you are in the center lane, then you should make an effort to move over to the right lane even knowing that you'll probably get back into that lane at an opportune time. Some state driver's manuals state that you should only drive in the left lane when you are passing another car, and otherwise you should be in the right lane. This is especially advised if there are only two lanes in each direction. Some states allow you to drive in the left lane at the speed limit if there are no cars for a considerable distance behind you. This assumes that you will be watching for that circumstance, and in my opinion, unless there are hazards in the right lane, you should ordinarily be in the right lane, or at least not in the left lane. Frequently cars come up very fast to pass in the left lane. An exception is when there are heavy rains or flooding or other weather conditions that necessitate you staying in the center or left lane which may be higher, with less water, and possibly less likely to cause hydroplaning. Again if there are cars trying to pass you, you should try to carefully move over to a right lane.

All of us have seen too many instances where drivers were driving the speed limit in the left lane, meanwhile dozens of cars behind them were weaving in and out trying to get past them, and the driver was definitely not conscious of the fact that he or she was creating a traffic hazard. We have all seen instances where cars were tailgating the slower car in the left lane (not a good idea) trying to give them a message, which they almost never seem to get. *Slow cars in the left lane are a distinct hazard.*

A car that is merging should ideally accelerate up to the speed of the flow of traffic that they are merging into, rather than slowing down, but situations sometimes can dictate another approach. When there is a car entering an expressway trying to merge, if you see the car is going very slowly, then use your judgment, because that car might be expecting you to get ahead and that is one of the areas that is difficult and most drivers develop judgment. If there is a question, caution is best. Often if you slow down, the entering driver will realize that you are allowing them to enter.

Again remember there is a vast difference between "yield" which means slowing down and stopping if necessary, and "merge" which encourages you to build up speed and to enter without slowing down or stopping unless necessary.

If you are driving in a particular lane and the white line on your left or right changes from intermittent to solid, you should ideally not change lanes at that point. You should do this ordinarily only when the solid line has again changed to an intermittent line. If circumstances do necessitate going over a solid white line, do so with greatly increased caution. These laws may vary from state to state.

SUMMARY: Ordinarily you should avoid the left lane on a four or six lane highway unless you are passing other cars. Just because you are driving the speed limit doesn't give you the right to drive in the left lane. Slow cars in the left lane are a hazard. Ordinarily you should not cross a solid white line.

LANE CHANGING

Lane changing is safer if you have your mirrors set properly, and you need to always know what's on each side of you, behind you, and in front of you, particularly on the side into which lane you are going to change. Be sure that there is no car in your way or coming up very fast. Be aware that the car behind you or two lanes over may try to enter the same lane that you are intending to enter.

There is an often-heard caution that if you turn your head in a certain direction, the tendency is to steer the car in that direction. Most drivers actually learn how to correct for that early on, but initially beginners should be careful as they twist or turn their head around to look for traffic, i.e. not to turn the wheel in the same direction until you intend to move in that direction.

It is important when you change lanes to not only check the side and rear view mirrors, but also to look to the left or right even beyond the pillar separating the front and rear windows. You can even lean forward looking into the left side view mirror to try to eliminate or at least lessen the blind spot.

If you hear a horn honk, be aware that another driver may be trying to alert you of the danger of an improper change or an impending collision and you may wish to abort your intention to change lanes.

> **Do not assume that just putting on your turn signal gives you the privilege of changing lanes if there is not a safe opening.**

Some newer cars offer as an option or standard equipment a blind spot indicator, i.e. alerting the driver that there is a car, and some indicate even a bicycle, in their blind spot. While that might turn out to be a welcome supplement to good driving technique, it is not a substitute for that, and may not be totally reliable. Be both alert and courteous to other drivers who may be using right or left turn signals if they are also changing lanes. Try to accommodate them if possible, especially if a car is trying to merge into lanes or trying to move over to make a right or a left turn, or to exit a freeway or expressway.

I have found that if you are right next to a car, it is often difficult to predict their needs and for that reason it would eventually be helpful if all cars had directional turn signals on their side view mirrors, as some cars have now.

If I am being tailgated by a heavy truck in the middle lane, I'll usually move over to one of the other lanes. The middle lane might be the trucks passing lane and if you are not going as fast as the truck, then you especially need to move out of that lane. I'm also not particularly comfortable being between two large trucks, although often in heavy traffic, I as well as others, find that that's pretty much where we are for part of the journey. Maintaining a safe interval behind the truck in front of you is one safety measure in that situation.

When changing lanes, be certain that the car that will be in front of you in the lane that you are entering is traveling at a fast enough speed and not slowing down or stopping.

Remember that motorcycles, short cars, and in some instances bicycles can be in your blind spot and may not be seen as easily as a regular sized car.

SUMMARY: When changing lanes, check not only the rear and side view mirrors but also look to the left or right, even beyond the pillar separating the front and rear windows. Be courteous, try to accommodate other drivers who are trying to change lanes in order to exit. The two right lanes might be the ones that trucks are asked to stay in. If you are in the center lane of three lanes, and if you are being tailgated by a truck, or you know that the truck wants to pass, then you should move over.

PASSING

O N A FOUR OR MORE LANE highway, with two or more lanes in each direction, generally you can pass on either side, although it is generally considered safer to pass on the left.

It is illegal to pull off of the paved road in order to pass a car on their right, and this ordinarily would most likely be relating to passing a car that was slowing or stopped to turn left into a driveway or an alley or a residential street. It is illegal to use the shoulder to pass a car or truck.

When passing, you need to be certain that you are not in a no passing zone as indicated by markings on the road, or by signs, or both. **Also never pass approaching the top of a hill or curve unless it is a four or six lane highway.**

When passing a car or a truck, pass rather quickly, however not exceeding the speed limit. This may be especially true in regards to a large truck which has a large blind spot and you don't want to be in that blind spot any longer then you have to be. It is also a good idea to not drive in the blind spot of any vehicle and this means usually not being almost even or actually slightly behind the car in an adjacent lane, because the cars' pillars separating the front seat from the back seat of the car in the adjacent lane may cause a substantial blind spot.

> **After passing either a car or truck, it is important to be sure that you can see the *entire front of the vehicle in your rear view mirror* before you signal and begin to carefully move back into their lane.**

If you are the car or truck being passed, don't accelerate, possibly even slow down a little to allow the passing vehicle to safely cut back into your lane, and this is especially important on a two-lane highway.

SUMMARY: Never pass approaching the top of a hill or curve unless it is a four or six lane highway. It is a good idea when passing another vehicle, especially a large truck, to do it rather quickly so that you don't remain in their blind spot any longer then necessary.

SHARING THE ROAD WITH TRUCKS

ACCIDENTS INVOLVING TRUCKS CAN BE DEADLY for many reasons, not the least of which is the size of most trucks, their greater weight and lesser maneuverability, and their longer braking distance.

While most truck drivers are responsible and very often the best drivers on the road, a small but significant and definitely bothersome percentage of truck drivers do unsafe things (drive recklessly, tailgate and thus intimidate other drivers, speed, drive in restricted lanes, and in other ways create hazards). Some tragic truck accidents are the result of truckers being drowsy, probably driving too long or not having enough sleep before driving, or both. There are regulations in this regard but sometimes they are not closely followed.

> When semi-trailer trucks try to stop suddenly, sometimes because they are cut off by another car or truck, or for other reasons including shifting of cargo, they may jackknife or roll over creating a very dangerous situation for everyone in the area. This may happen especially on slippery roads, but even in dry weather.

There is a danger of objects falling off of or out of trucks. You should be able to spot a truck that has a number of items on it that seem to not be properly secured. That's a good truck to avoid being anywhere near. The most frequent items falling off of trucks are ladders, but pallets, steel coils or any load can fall off or out.

> **Anything that falls off of or spills out of a truck in front of you becomes a dangerous obstacle in the road. This is another reason to keep a safe interval between you and the truck in front of you.**

If you are behind a tall truck, a traffic light might not be visible to you until you are practically at, or actually into, or even through an intersection. Now the traffic lights are not only on the corners, but often also in the center of the intersection on horizontal supports, and that makes it less likely that this will happen, but one should still be alert to this possibility.

When you are on an expressway, highway, or freeway, and you are trying to read signs, particularly exit signs, a truck can obscure those, and if you are too close behind a truck, you usually won't have time to read the signs. If you are in the lane to the left of the truck, you might also miss the sign entirely. Therefore, if you need to see signs or to exit, then you need to be far enough behind or ahead of the truck to make it possible to see the signs and to read them at highway speeds. A GPS may also help you in this regard.

If you can't see the truck driver in their mirror, the driver can't see you. If you can't see the mirror at all, then there is obviously no chance that the driver can see you. There can be blind spots on both sides of the truck and for quite a distance behind a large truck. When you are about to pass a truck on a two lane highway, if there is no opposing traffic, briefly flashing your lights as a signal that you are passing is advised by many. Some also would advise the trucker to flash his lights, after you have passed, acknowledging that you can safely move back into that lane in front of him.

If you are being seriously tailgated by a truck, or you see someone else being tailgated for more than just a brief distance, if you have a passenger, they could use a cell phone to call * 999 to alert authorities and give a description of the truck. The same is true if you see a trucker driving in the wrong lane for a considerable distance or at an excessive speed. As always, try to avoid any instance of road rage, and by all means avoid being distracted.

I have occasionally seen large semi-trailer trucks driving two or three abreast, on a four or six lane highway, and these trucks were not even related to each other, i.e. not from the same company, but they were keeping the same speed so that no one could pass. That's another situation which should be reported to authorities, if it goes on for any length of time or distance.

> **Even if you are keeping a safe distance from the car in front of you, and you realize that you have to stop suddenly, if there is a truck behind you, it may not be able to stop, so make sure you are familiar with the shoulder, because that can be an emergency escape route.**

Listening to the radio traffic reports will often alert you when a truck has hit a bridge abutment, or has misjudged the height of an underpass and has become stuck under it, blocking the lane or causing even a more serious traffic disruption. Truck drivers ordinarily would be aware of the height of their truck, and thereby avoid going underneath a bridge or any other structure that will cause them to become stuck. Being stuck under a bridge not only damages the property and holds up traffic for hours, but can even cause problems in the area for days or weeks while the damage is being repaired. This does happen with surprising frequency.

With snow in the winter, or even with rain at other times of the year, there can be a considerable spray of water or snow coming off of a truck, which could land on your windshield unless you stay far enough behind so that this does not become a problem. This same can be true even *following* rain or snow. The tires from a truck may kick up dirt, water, and snow and this could be a hazard for any vehicle that is following too closely. If something does come off of a truck, or even if you see any other item coming toward you, it is usually better not to swerve, unless you are certain there is nothing in the way. It may be safer to continue straight or to stop if possible. If something such as a tire or wheel is bouncing up and down, you may need to duck down in case it hits the windshield.

> **Trucks and buses often have to make especially wide right and even sharp left turns. If a truck is turning right, they will often move somewhat to the left, even outside of the right turn lane, in order to make their turn. There may be a sign on the back of the truck that says "*Caution, Makes Wide Right Turns*," or you may just simply be aware that large trucks often may have to do that. Never try to pass on the right side in that situation and allow the truck or bus plenty of room. If you see that a large truck or bus is turning left or right, into the street that you are coming to a stop at, hang back a little to give them a little extra leeway.**

Buses, including school buses and others that carry passengers for hire, as well as trucks that are carrying hazardous or flammable contents, and sometimes other vehicles, will automatically stop at railroad crossings. Remember that sudden braking or turning of larger trucks can cause the cargo to shift, and that's another reason that semis might jackknife or roll-over even on a dry road.

Mail trucks and delivery trucks such as FedEx and UPS are more likely to pull out from parking or double parked spots because they are making short runs.

Never try to squeeze past a truck that might be backing up or partly obstructing the road. Stop and be patient until you are certain what the situation is. Remember the truck driver can not see what is directly behind him or her in most instances.

Some trailer trucks that are pulling a long flat bed, either loaded or empty, and some long car transporters, might have difficulty in keeping the flat bed or car transporter in their lane, especially around curves. Be cautious and pick a safe opportunity to pass if necessary.

Do not stop too close behind a cement mixer truck, since sometimes the chute can flip down. A truck may roll back before going forward after stopping on a hill. Be alert and allow extra space.

Be aware of trucks carrying high pressure gas cylinders. If they become involved in a crash or overturn, the gas cylinders can explode, causing a horrendous fire, and the cylinders themselves may act as missiles traveling either through the air some distance, or even in both directions of that side of the highway, s well as crossing into the opposing traffic. Keep a considerable distance behind such a truck, and if you come across an accident involving that type of situation, avoid getting anywhere near it.

> **Be aware that heavy trucks will slow down going up hills, and will speed up going down hills. A car may easily pass trucks going uphill on a four lane highway, but they should be very cautious and generally should avoid trying to pass a truck going downhill, particularly on a two lane highway.**

RAILROAD CROSSINGS

M OST RAILROAD CROSSINGS ARE MARKED WITH a round yellow sign that has a large X on it, and they may have an RR as well. Many, but not all track crossings are also protected by gates, and all track crossings should have signals. There may be a sign that says "Train Has No Horn." If there is any question that a signal light or gate isn't working and a train may be approaching, stop, look, listen and then proceed extremely cautiously. At night, the lights of a train usually can be seen from a distance. It is better to turn off your radio, open your window so that you can hear, and be prepared to stop if necessary. Always report a railroad crossing signal that is out of order or a gate that is not functioning. Crossings with obstructive views are especially dangerous.

> **Never try to beat a train to a railroad crossing. Come to a complete stop if the light signal is flashing, and ascertain the situation. You need to stop between 15 and 50 feet from the nearest track.**

If the gate is down and/or the signals are malfunctioning, and you don't see a train approaching after a reasonable period of time, then you should call * 999, or even better, 9-1-1 to report that. Generally assistance will come and direct traffic appropriately, and the police can also contact the railroad authorities who can directly contact the conductor of approaching trains to be on increased alert. It could take a train a full mile to stop.

> **You should never go around a gate that has been lowered.**

If you find yourself waiting in a long line and there is no train, or the train seems to be stuck, many drivers will do a three-point turn, since there will be little if any traffic in the opposing lane or lanes, and they will go back and find another way to cross the track at some other point, such as an over or under pass. Drivers who are waiting will often turn off their motor.

> **It is extremely important to know the length of the vehicle that you are driving, especially if it is a bus or truck, and no matter what you are driving, do not cross the tracks unless you are totally certain there is adequate space for you on the other side to completely clear the tracks.**

It is a good idea to shift to a lower gear *before* you go over rough or bumpy tracks, especially if you have a manual gear shift. Never shift gears as you are going over the tracks.

> **If you do happen to get stuck on the tracks for whatever reason, get out of your car and run far away from the tracks in the direction that the train is approaching from, or run perpendicular to the tracks. That way, if your car is struck by the train, debris will be flung in the direction away from you. If you have your cell phone with you, notify the authorities by calling 9-1-1.**

Remember that a second train may follow, and a train may be coming from the other direction. There have been rare instances where a car waiting at railroad crossing gates was struck from behind and pushed into a moving train. If you are the lead car stopped at crossing gates, be sure to stop behind the white stop line, and keep your eye on your mirror to be certain the car following you is stopping. If it appears that it isn't, brake hard with regular and emergency brakes and be sure the top of your head does not come above your head rest (to minimize the risk of whiplash). My wife stops even further behind the white line, to prevent being hit from behind and pushed into the train's path. Another advantage of stopping further away is to be out of the path of a derailed or overturned railroad car, especially those that are very tall, and also those that may be carrying flammable contents. Some railroad cars extend up to several feet on either side of the tracks.

EMERGENCY VEHICLES

(Fire Trucks, Ambulances, Police Cars and other emergency vehicles including Department of Transportation trucks.)

I F YOU HEAR A SIREN, OR you even think you hear a siren, turn off your radio, and also the heater or air conditioner if it is making substantial noise, and ask your passengers, if any, to not talk or make noise until you determine if there is an emergency vehicle in the area. It is important in the modern air-tight cars to crack the window, especially on the driver's side, or even both front windows. If you put the windows all the way down, you will hear even better.

> **If you see an emergency vehicle in your rear view mirror, or your side view mirror, either to the left or right, or in front of you, then you need to pull over safely to the right as far as possible and stop. If you can't pull over, then at least stop where you are, and give the emergency vehicle the opportunity to know where you are and what you are going to do, i.e. stay where you are until it or they have passed. Remember there may be multiple emergency vehicles of different types and they may be coming from several directions.**

If you are reasonably certain that you are hearing an emergency vehicle, but you can't tell where it is coming from, it is still a good idea to pull over and stop and put your flashers on to let other cars know that you are stopping, and perhaps alert them to the possibility of an approaching emergency vehicle. Try to leave enough space between your car and the car in front of you, so that a car that needs to pull over can also get out of the way of the emergency vehicle.

If you are on a clearly divided highway with substantial distance between the two directions of lanes, especially separated by a barrier such as a cement divider, or an unpaved surface five feet wide, although you might reasonably slow down, you don't need to stop if there is an emergency vehicle approaching you from the opposite direction. However, if you are approaching an intersection, you should stop, because the emergency vehicle or vehicles might be turning in front of you at that point, or might even need to cross into your lane to get by an obstruction in their direction.

> **You should be aware that there may be other emergency vehicles coming from any direction and the emergency vehicles may have to go down the wrong side of the road to get around stopped traffic to get to an emergency site.**

Be alert to any possibility. Occasionally, the only way an emergency vehicle can get through an intersection is by pulling up behind you, especially if you are in the left lane, and then blasting their horn. If that happens, don't panic, just try to move out of the way by pulling around the car on your right, if necessary pulling slightly into the crosswalk or even part way into the intersection to allow the emergency vehicles to get through or to turn.

If you are talking on a hands-free cell phone and you think you hear an emergency vehicle, tell the party that you have to get off the phone immediately because of an emergency vehicle, and that you will call back as soon as you find a safe spot to do that. If you can't do that, tell whoever you are talking to on a hands free phone to not speak until the emergency vehicle has passed.

> **There is a small flashing white light at some intersections, a foot or two from the traffic lights on the horizontal pole that extends over the intersection. This small flashing bright light indicates an approaching emergency vehicle, and may also trigger the red traffic light. Remember if the emergency vehicle is approaching toward you on the other side of the road, *unless* it is a clearly divided highway with *no* nearby intersections, you should still pull over to the side and stop.**

A bright flashing white light indicates an
emergency vehicle is approaching,

Be aware of the location of police stations and especially fire stations, since vehicles may pull out from them suddenly. There should be signaling devices indicating that an emergency vehicle is about to pull out. Be aware that diagonally and sometimes vertically or horizontally placed white lines often mark an area outside of a fire station indicating that you shouldn't stop in that area, in case the vehicles have to leave on an emergency call.

Drive very carefully near police cars that are stopped or other emergency vehicles that have stopped to assist a stalled motorist or an accident. Move over to a further lane if possible.

> **It's the law in most, if not all, states that you must move over to another lane further away when approaching a police car involved in a traffic stop, or for that matter any emergency vehicle. If you can't change lanes, go very, very slowly past the police car or another emergency vehicle.**

This "Move Over Law" is called "Scott's Law" in Illinois, named in memory of Chicago Fire Department Lt. Scott Gillen, who tragically was fatally injured by a drunken driver while working at a crash on the Bishop Ford Freeway in the year 2000. Lt. Gillen was 37, and the father of five children.

In any accident or fire, or any police or other emergency activity, be alert for other emergency vehicles arriving or leaving, such as police cars, ambulances, fire trucks, and tow trucks. If there are authorities that are handling traffic, obey their directions.

Always remember that if you see one police or other emergency vehicle, there could be others just seconds behind it, or even coming from other directions. Police cars that are responding to a burglary will often have their siren off and use only their flashing lights, and that's another reason you need to look at your mirrors routinely. Watch for responding police cars which also may be coming from several directions. Police cars and even fire rescue trucks, often follow an ambulance on the way to a medical emergency or to a hospital.

Be aware of the danger of being hit by a car speeding while being pursued by a police car, and there is also the danger of being hit by a police car or another emergency vehicle itself.

Always give emergency vehicles the courtesy and respect that you would want if you were the driver, the passenger, or the patient, or in the case of an accident, the victim awaiting emergency assistance, or the resident of a dwelling on fire or involved in any other emergency. Being able to be aware of emergency vehicles is another reason to keep the noise level down inside the car. For those who are hearing impaired, the visual awareness becomes even more important. Keeping the window cracked slightly, or even open when the weather or driving conditions permit, is also helpful.

Remember, if you are caught where you can't pull over, just stay where you are and the emergency vehicle may go in the opposing lane to get past you.

DRIVING AWARENESS, ANTICIPATION AND "BAD DRIVER" AVOIDANCE

THIS CHAPTER NECESSARILY INCLUDES SOME REFERENCES to courtesy. A heightened sense of awareness is one of the keys to safer driving. It is also a key to more courteous and responsible driving.

> A good motto is "*expect the unexpected*," and you will encounter this so often, that you could easily change the motto to "*expect the expected*."

Although you might eventually learn to somewhat predict the moves a car is going to make, and you should try to develop this feeling intuitively, you should not rely completely on this. Rather, rely on your own driving skills and your defensive driving ability.

Methodically monitoring your mirrors so that you are always aware of what's behind you, and what's on either side of you as well as what is in front of you is the key. If a ball, Frisbee, or any other similar object, rolls, bounces, or flys into the street, it is likely to be followed by a small child, or in some instances by a pet dog. If a dog or cat runs into the street, it could very well be followed by its owner, which could also be a child.

If you are stuck behind a car that doesn't seem to be moving, or seems to be stalled, stay behind it for a few seconds until you are reasonably certain that the driver is not going to make a sudden move in either direction. If you decide to carefully pull around it, a very slight beep of your horn might be indicated to be sure that they know where you are so they don't turn into you. If their emergency flashers are on, or their hood is up, or both, and they are stopped, they are less likely to move or turn.

If you notice a car in front of you or in an adjacent lane stopping or pulling over, be aware that there is most likely some legitimate reason. There may be someone crossing the street that you haven't yet seen, or a pet has run into the street, or the driver in front of you may have become aware of an approaching emergency vehicle before you can see or hear it. A car that is stopping in an unusual place might very well be allowing another car to enter or exit a parking lot, driveway, alley, or an intersection. Although it may not always be true, just assume that a car (or cars) stopping in an unusual place, has a good reason, and be prepared to stop.

When you are driving in areas of high residential density, such as townhouses or apartments, especially areas where they may not have garages, driveways, or alleys in which to park, be aware that the resident's cars are often parked on the street. The owners may be in or near the street, washing or maintaining their cars. They may get in and out of their car on the driver's side. There may even be a fence on the passenger side of those parked cars, so be particularly cautious in these areas, and allow a little extra space on your car's right side (and left side too).

Good drivers often learn to anticipate (but not completely trust) other drivers' intentions and/or actions, based on speed, consistency, body movement, and other subtle factors.

Don't always trust another car's turn signal, because the car may or may not be turning. Drivers coming out of or into a half or angle turn may forget to turn their signal off. The same may be true of drivers who have used turn signals before a lane change, expressway exit or entrance. Newer motorcycles may have turn signals which automatically turn off.

Driving defensively means that you are driving at a speed at which you have control, even if someone else does the unexpected. It means that you have a great awareness of what is around you.

It is important to be aware of motorcycles and bicyclists. They are harder to see and you have to keep looking in your mirror and you should get in the habit of continuously alerting yourself to their possible presence. In some business districts in large cities in our country, messenger bicyclists may come up very fast from behind, or may be hidden in a blind spot, and often drive in a hurried and seemingly unsafe fashion.

> **Always look carefully before you pull around another car or change lanes, or exit your car.**

Motorcycles ordinarily have their headlight on, but motorcycles are often short enough to be easily hidden in a blind spot. Often they, as will bicyclists, drive between two cars in adjacent lanes, even though that is illegal. Speeding motorcyclists often cut in and out of lanes, narrowly missing cars. Some of the newer shorter cars also may be easily hidden in your blind spot.

When driving alongside parked cars, watch for slightly open or opening car doors, and turning front wheels. Try not to block exits or entrances to parking lots or alleys, or businesses, including filling stations.

> **Cars that violate the law by weaving or cutting off other cars, or speeding, or changing lanes without signaling, are likely to continue to drive in that fashion and therefore you must show extreme caution and keep a safe distance usually behind such a driver.**

If a car is banged up, or "taped together," this may be an unfortunate driver who hasn't yet had the time or the funds to repair it. It may also signify that this is a bad driver that you need to avoid. The same could be said of a car that is so covered with road dust, dirt or snow that the driver's visibility is hampered. Be cautious with drivers that are driving unusually slow, or straying over the line, or are obviously on their cell phone or texting or falling asleep or intoxicated. It is probably best to stay behind at a safe distance until you figure out a safe course of action, which might be to pass them with a wide margin.

If a driver is unusually slow to start when a traffic light changes, or has left an excessive interval between their car and the car in front at a traffic light, they are likely to be unfocused, visually impaired, distracted or just incompetent, and hence present greater danger to nearby drivers. They also might still be learning to drive properly. Be wary of drivers who go from one side of their lane to the other, or drift over into another lane. They may be on a cell phone, drowsy, or intoxicated.

There is one intersection, actually a "T" intersection in a Chicago suburb, which has had a pattern of infractions. Cars stopped at a stop sign at the end of the road, then entering the intersection to turn right or left, would often pull out right in front of me or other cars. It has happened so regularly (possibly because of the configuration of the stop line, the cross traffic, and trees and bushes obstructing vision) that I use great caution. Be aware that sometimes, particularly in certain areas where you might frequently drive, other drivers might almost predictably make unexpected and potentially dangerous moves.

PARKING

PARKING HAS CONSIDERABLE TO DO WITH safety, and a lot to do with courtesy. There are different types of parking situations, notably, indoor parking lots, outdoor parking lots, parallel parking, and angle or straight-in parking.

Most drivers have been taught and will have practiced parallel parking in the course of their instruction. I would only add the importance of remembering if you are backing into a parallel parking space, as you turn the steering wheel to the right, i.e. clockwise, that pulls the front left end of your car out further. If it is a narrow street, and a car is coming toward you, or if a car is passing you, wait until either car passes. The car behind you might stop, indicating that they are allowing you to back-up, in which case you would carefully do that if you will not hit or block an opposing car. It is also true in multi-lane traffic, in other words, when there are two or more lanes going in each direction, you want to be certain that you are not creating a situation by putting the front end of your car across the lane line as you back up, which could cause a car in the lane next to you to veer to their left.

Parallel parking becomes more difficult because of the way most modern cars are built. Generally, in older cars you could see both the front and back end of the car, but in more modern cars, usually you can't see either, and you just develop a feel for where the front and rear are. This is different from car to car and when you are driving a car that you are not familiar with, you have to be especially careful in this regard. When going forward or backing up, especially as you are developing that feel, go very slowly so that if you do happen to touch the car in front or in back of you, you hopefully won't damage it. I find that I generally underestimate the distance to the car behind me and sometimes even in front of me. It's helpful to get out and compare what you thought was the distance to the actual distance, and eventually modify or correct your distance estimating ability. You can tell how close you are to the curb by using the right side view mirror.

One trick that I discovered a few years ago is that if you are parallel parking and there are stores with plate glass windows adjacent to where you are parking, frequently you can see the reflection of your car, as well as that of the parked cars in front and in back of you, in the window. This is probably most helpful in knowing how far back to go. Parking assist features and rear view cameras make this easier.

> **Always when parking, think of the Golden Rule. Do unto others as you would have them do unto you. Treat the car next to you as you would want your car treated if the situation was reversed. Be careful in a parking lot that you don't hit the car next to you with your door. This is especially true if it is windy, in which case you should firmly grasp and hold your door as you are opening it so that it doesn't catch the wind and swing out wide and dent the car next to you.**

Dents are expensive to repair, and when side mirrors are damaged, they are also expensive to repair or replace, especially the electrically operated remote controlled side view mirrors. Often car doors will open up to a point, and then to a second point, but even if you know that the door may go to one of these points, it is still a good idea to hold onto the door as you are opening it so that under no circumstance does it swing out and hit the car next to you.

If you are angle parking or parking in a lot where the spaces are straight forward, i.e. straight-in, remember when you leave, as you back up and turn the wheel to the right or left, the front end of your car again comes out to either the left or the right, so you want to be sure that you don't hit the car on either side. Again practice and experience will help in this regard.

Parking next to a new or expensive and/or well-maintained car is less likely to result in damage to your car, as opposed to parking next to a banged up car. The person driving a well-maintained car probably is conscientious in taking care of their car, and likely will be careful not to damage the cars next to them.

You should also be aware when parking, that two-door cars, including convertibles, have especially wide doors, and if they swing open and out, they will cover a greater distance. If you are trying to be especially careful, you would park next to smaller four door cars. The attitude of the driver and passengers in adjacent cars is probably more important then the type of car.

Many drivers have tried to protect their car by parking in a remote area of a parking lot, somewhere away from where other cars are parked. Often they come out to find that there is a car parked right next to their car. Although they might be upset at that, usually the person who has parked next to their car is aware that they have parked in a remote area to avoid being dented by an adjacent car, and they will likely show the same concern and respect.

> **For safety considerations, it may sometimes be important to *not* park in remote and/or dimly lit areas of a parking lot.**

When parking, be certain that you don't occupy a parking space reserved for a person with a disability unless you are legally authorized to do so. If you are driving a car that has a person with a disability license, but you are not that person, that doesn't qualify, unless the person with a disability is a passenger. Save those spots for people who really need them. There are stiff penalties in many states for people who violate this, including for physicians who authorize persons for disability parking when it is not medically justifiable.

When you pull into a covered parking lot, i.e. an indoor parking lot, whether it is daytime or nighttime, make certain that you put your lights on. Many cars have automatic headlights but sometimes there is a delay before they go on.

> **It is important to turn your lights on as soon as you enter the parking lot to make sure you are visible to other drivers, especially those who might be backing up to exit. Remember to turn them off after parking, if this is not automatic.**

You can often tell if a car is about to move, especially backing up, if you see the wheels turn, or if the back-up lights go on, or you can see the driver turning the wheel, or even buckling their seat belt. It is important to go slow in parking lots to avoid even low speed collisions. If you are in a parking lot and you hear a horn, it may be that someone is trying to avoid an accident, so stop and try to ascertain where it is coming from. This is one instance where use of the horn is reasonable to alert someone, although the brake is an even better tool. If someone is backing up and they can't or don't see you, then either stop and allow them to go, or if you are already in their path, honk your horn. Sometimes, after I have backed up a foot or so, I see back up lights come on in the cars parked behind me. I may choose to pull back into my parking spot to avoid a fender or bumper bender.

If, when parallel parking, after getting out of the car, you realize that you are over a foot away from the curb, you need to safely get back in the car and gradually get closer, and that involves a skill that an instructor will teach you. Generally, it is pulling forward as far as you can, and then turning the steering wheel to the right and then back to the left as you back up to get even closer to the curb. You might have to do that entire maneuver eight or ten times to get close enough, depending upon how much space you have between the two cars you are parked between and how far you were from the curb to start. Although some states say a foot from the curb is acceptable, if you are that far away from the curb, you could be obstructing traffic in the lane next to you and you could put your car at risk, as well as other drivers. Generally speaking, I would recommend that you try to be no more than four to six inches from a curb. Wider cars need to be closer to the curb. With parallel parking, if there are spaces marked for each car, after you parked, once outside the car you see that your front or back end is over the line, safely get back in and put your car inside the marked space. If you are in a parking lot and you get out and see that you are over the marked lines, or that you are too close to a car on one side, you should get back into the car and try to put the car in a more central position, unless the cars on either side have not parked centrally, in which case you may have to modify your actions. There are some drivers who will intentionally straddle a line knowing that they won't leave enough room for another car to park, possibly on either side of them. That's not only discourteous, but also selfish.

When parking in an indoor parking lot with many levels, remember that if you are parking on an up or down ramp, there is a greater chance that when the driver next to you gets out, or even the passenger gets out, that the door will be pulled by gravity into your car. If you can park on a level space, you are less likely to face that problem. There is a difference in the ramps between being at risk from the driver's side and being at risk from the passenger side. Consider what the situation is, i.e. is this a place for shoppers, in which case often there will just be the driver, or is this a sporting or other family oriented event in which case often there will be several passengers, possibly entire families.

> **Parking on an inclined ramp, whether it is going up or down, is another instance where you might need to grab hold of the car door as you open it so that gravity doesn't cause the door to strike the car next to you.**

From a safety point of view, in regards to parking, especially in walking to enter your car, walk confidently, briskly, and don't be burdened down with an over abundance of packages. Keep your eyes open for any suspicious activity. Perhaps especially at night, and in lonely locations, from a distance, check to be sure no one is hiding under your car, if your car has a high clearance, such as an SUV or pick-up truck might have. When you get close to the car, look inside to be sure that there is no one inside the car, inside the back seat, or if there has been any tampering or damage to the car. With any of these circumstances, if you have the slightest suspicion, return to the store or office and obtain security to walk you back to your car, or notify the police.

Remember that women particularly, but sometimes men also, have a tendency to get into their car after shopping, eating, or working, and sometimes they just sit there, possibly looking over their checkbook, or making a list, or just getting their thoughts together. Predators could be watching, and this could be a perfect opportunity for a predator to get in and endanger you.

Lock the car doors as soon as you get in, start your car, and don't unnecessarily linger in that area, unless there is considerable traffic and it is a very well lit area with evident security. If you have to leave quickly because of any perceived or real danger, you'll be prepared to do that.

Watch carefully for pedestrians in parking lots, because as you are backing up, it is hard to see a person who is walking, and they may not notice you. If you just back up slowly, a little bit at a time, a few inches to start, then that increases the safety aspect greatly.

Also be aware that at times, and I've seen this often, parents will push a stroller with an infant often as much as 20 feet ahead of them in a parking lot. They would then catch up with the stroller, apparently thinking that the act is amusing for the child. Unfortunately, they lose all control of the stroller and there could be a car backing up, and this is another reason to be very careful. Many cars do have back up cameras, and others have sensing devices such as buzzers, but even then there are limitations and distractions, and it's best to just ease very slowly as you back up, especially in a parking lot. Be especially watchful for small children and disabled persons.

Parents should hold onto the hands of small children when walking to or from their car in parking lots.

Most of us are aware that many trucks often make loud beeping sounds when they are backing up, to alert others, particularly pedestrians.

In some parking lots, where there are relatively blind corners, there may be convex mirrors mounted to help you see around corners. Keep an eye out for these mirrors, proceed slowly, always looking for other cars, and again always keep your lights on in an indoor parking lot. It is a good idea to keep your lights on in an outdoor parking lot as well, even during daylight. You do need to remember to turn them off, especially if you don't have an automatic shut off.

As a courtesy, if you are parking at a sporting event or concert or other outdoor parking lot where you may be directed to pull alongside another just parked car, if the person or persons in the car which preceded you haven't yet exited, wait a minute until they do exit so that the two of you don't open at the same time and bang car doors.

When you are in a parking lot and you are backing up or pulling forward, if you are next to a van or an SUV, you may not be able to see as easily as you could if you were next to a regular sedan. Again just be cautious and go slowly.

When you are in a parking lot where there are aisles of cars, and you are backing up, the car in the aisle behind you may also be backing up, and the two of you could hit each other. Be alert, watching in your mirrors and through the back window for back up lights, and always go slow, continuously checking your mirrors and looking through the back and side windows.

In some parking areas, you may be able to park up against a curb or a fence at the end of an aisle, where there is no parking aisle directly behind you. This eliminates or decreases the chance of a car backing into you as they are leaving.

When you are in a parking lot, either indoors or outdoors, notice if there is some type of a concrete curb or other barrier that your front wheels might be up against. I've come out of stores not realizing this and have gotten into my car thinking that I had the opportunity to pull forward, which is usually easier than backing up, and was embarrassed to realize that I was hitting a curb or parking barrier. It is a good idea as you get out of the car to make a mental note of this, and as you walk back to the car to also observe not only anything in front of you, but also if there is any obstacle behind you.

Always remember that back up lights are white and not colored.

If you have small articles in the car, especially if they are dark, and if you have sunglasses on, when you pull into a parking lot, especially one that is underground, or one with poor lighting, you might not notice those items as you get out. You might need some of them, or you might not want to leave certain objects visible to others.

> In parking lots, pedestrians, who may be within seconds or minutes of becoming drivers, are walking to or from their car, and are often distracted by using cell phones, or they may be in areas where there are no sidewalks, and people may cross streets in shopping mall parking lots without concern for traffic. There may be pedestrians who are actually intoxicated, "walking under the influence" (WUI). *Be aware, go slow, and always give the pedestrian the right-of-way.*

In a paid parking lot, usually you take your ticket with you and note if you should pay on exiting the facility or as you reenter before you get to your car. Some will allow you to pay at the exit gate. In some instances, you can have your parking ticket validated at a doctors office, restaurant, or other business or store to decrease or eliminate the parking fee altogether. It is a good idea, especially in a multi-level parking lot, to mark the location, which usually means the floor and the aisle, so there will often be a number and a letter, and also often another number to help you find your car in a particular section. You can put this on your ticket just to remind you so that you don't have a problem finding your car when you are leaving. If you have difficulty finding your car, and you have a remote fob, try holding it up high and pressing "unlock" or even the panic button to aid you in locating your car. Elevators are considered safer than stairwells.

When you are exiting a parking lot, or even entering it, and a car is trying to back up to get into an aisle to exit, it is customary courtesy to allow the car to back up in order to get in line to exit. In parking lots especially watch for persons with disabilities, elderly persons or children.

> As you are exiting a parking space it is a good idea to not only back up slowly, but also to keep your radio off and your windows cracked open so that you can hear a horn honking or any other indication that you need to stop. If there is a safety concern, keep the windows closed. Ask passengers to hold off on conversation, as you proceed slowly and cautiously to leave the parking space and the lot.

If you leave your car at a nightclub or restaurant or hotel where there is valet parking, make certain the valet is someone who really represents or works for the organization, hotel, club, or restaurant. If you have a valet key, use that or a fob when you turn your key over to the valet, and don't leave your house or work keys on the ring. I routinely lock my trunk and glove compartment and try not to leave important or valuable items loose in the car. Although the vast majority of valet and parking attendants are honest, the extra measure can't hurt. Access to the trunk behind a folding arm rest in the back seat can often be locked with the car key.

Some cars offer parking assist options and some can even indicate whether a space is large enough for your car. While this option will help you put your car into the parking space, it may still be up to you in terms of pulling forward or backwards after you are once in the space, but some newer cars will do this as well.

TWO-WAY LEFT TURN LANES

THIS SPECIAL LANE IN THE CENTER of a street (either a two, three or four lane street) is indicated by separate arrows curving to the right and left. They are used for cars going in either direction to turn left into side streets or alleys, or parking lots.

Some states indicate that you shouldn't enter a two-way left turn lane until you are 200 feet away from where you are turning. Even within that distance, if there is another car coming from the *opposite* direction which is turning to *their left*, and you see them enter the lane, the best thing to do would be to slowly stop and see where they are going. If they are turning beyond you, that would suggest that you may have entered too early for the circumstances. You need to safely get back into the lane which is to your right, and then after passing the opposing car, reenter the two-way left turn lane. Frequently there may be offices, restaurants, and other business directly across from your intended entrance.

> Two-way left turn lanes should never be used for passing other cars, or for parking, except in some instances where construction or street maintenance leaves the "left turn only" or a two-way left turn lane as the "only" lane for passing the obstruction. I often see car transport trucks parked in a two-way turn left lane, unloading the transported cars, because that is the only place they can unload at that particular location.

OBSTRUCTIONS

THERE ARE MANY OBSTRUCTIONS THAT CAN be encountered on the roadway:

- the car in front of you
- wheels having come off of cars or trucks
- wheels with tires
- tires by themselves
- ladders (actually the most frequent item to fall off a truck)
- large rocks especially in mountainous or hilly areas
- dead or live animals
- children running into the roadway
- pedestrians
- bicycles
- motorcycles
- construction barriers
- accidents still on the road
- bridges that are out
- pot holes
- sewer covers that are raised during repaving (because the repaving is not yet finished with tapering around the edges of the sewer covers, leaving them still protruding up to an inch or so above the surface of the road, one of my pet peeves)
- piles of leaves in the fall and sometimes into the early winter
- mounds of snow, particularly plowed snow
- a ridge of ice around the outline of a car which was parked when the street was being plowed
- Roof carriers that have come off.

Report to *999 most obstructions that highway departments can remove.

Pot holes may be especially present in the winter with changes in temperature and ice and snow, but also in some years when pot holes are extensive, they may persist into the spring. Others drivers may swerve to avoid pot holes and that is another reason to keep a reasonable interval between the car in front of you. Hitting a pot hole can cause loss of control or can damage a tire, wheel or even the car itself. Braking just before a pot hole lowers the front end and may increase damage.

> **Pot holes are particularly tricky when it rains or snows because you can't tell how deep a pot hole is, if it is rain or snow filled.**

Pot holes are the cause of many flat tires and a driver should try to avoid hitting a pot hole. The most successful way is to be far enough behind the car in front and to be looking ahead and to also be very aware of what is on either side of you as well as in back of you. In that way, if you move or change lanes or swerve to avoid a pot hole, you will likely neither hit another car nor cause another car to be involved in a crash. If you have the space, and you see an object such as a pot hole, you can try to put it in the middle of the car as you go over it. If it is an object that has volume and extends upward, and you suspect that it is hard, firm or dense, then you may very well damage your car. If something appears suddenly, such as coming down a mountainside, then you might choose to veer, but you don't want to run off the mountain or hit another car head on, because that would very likely be more dangerous than hitting the obstacle.

In some climates, there can also be piles of leaves covered with snow.

Several years ago, while driving west on a busy street in Skokie, IL a large plastic tarp (sheet) flew off of the back of a truck and covered not only the front of my car including the engine compartment, but also the windshield. Some of it ended up tucked underneath the front of the car. I was able to pull into a parking lot, and remove all of the plastic sheet except for that which was under the car. My vision was only partially blocked since it was fairly clear vinyl plastic. I was worried about the car overheating and therefore stopped almost immediately. The dealership was able to remove the rest of it from underneath the car. Certainly a bizarre happening, but I share this with drivers so they will know to expect almost anything.

Truckers are encouraged to check their wheel lugs to be sure they are tight before and after each trip. Horrendous accidents have been caused by tires and entire wheels coming off of trucks especially, but they can also be a danger when coming off of a car.

Speed Bumps (Sometimes called Speed Humps)

Speed bumps are often put on residential streets or in parking lots to slow down traffic, and there should be signs alerting you to their upcoming presence, but these warnings are not always present. These elevations across the roadway often have red or black stripes or they may alternate with yellow, and can even at times be white. Sometimes the markings are in a diamond shape, with a diamond within a diamond, or a half diamond. Sometimes there are no markings at all. It is very important to slow down when encountering speed bumps for a number of reasons. First of all, going over a speed bump at anything over a few miles an hour will often cause damage to the car, and even loss of control. The purpose of the speed bump will be defeated if someone speeds over it, and pedestrians as well as others will be put at risk in such a situation, i.e. if you don't slow down appropriately.

> Speed bumps should be taken very seriously, and basically their presence means "SLOW DOWN." It is dangerous and usually illegal to speed up between speed bumps.

Rollerbladers and Skateboarders

Watch for rollerbladers and skateboarders going down either side of the street or cutting across the street in crosswalks. Apparently it is legal for people to be skating on some roadways, according to some state's rules of the road. Particularly watch for bicyclists coming down sidewalks, and rapidly entering crosswalks, unsuspected, often because of shrubbery or other visual obstructions.

Deer

Deer may be encountered near a road or a freeway, most often near dusk and dawn. You do however run a risk of encountering a deer at other hours of the day as well.

Deer may be found in wooded areas, rural areas, along highways, and even in suburban and urban areas. October through December is the most accident prone season for deer-vehicle collisions. Deer crossing the road may stop and even double back.

> **Usually braking hard is recommended instead of swerving if a deer is in your path.**

If a deer appears ahead of you, while slowing down, honk your horn with one long blast to try to frighten it away, and flash your lights. Unfortunately, high beams might freeze a deer also, so this could be a two edged sword.

It is generally recommended to avoid swerving if you encounter a deer since you could lose control of your car or hit another vehicle. Deer tend to travel in packs, so if you see one or several, slow down and let the deer continue on their path. Although high beam lights may freeze the deer, they also might illuminate the animal's eyes so that you can spot them sooner. Once you are aware of their presence, you should switch to low beams, if at night. It is recommended after you pass a herd of deer or any other obstruction or condition on the road, to alert drivers coming in the opposite direction by flashing your bright lights on and off at a safe distance (500 feet). Remember that it is illegal to flash your lights to warn oncoming drivers of policemen waiting for those who disobey speed laws.

If you do hit a deer, don't touch it because an injured or frightened deer might further injure itself or hurt you. It is advised to get your car off the road if possible, and notify the authorities. This same advice applies to any other large animal that may wander into or cross the road. If you take your car off the road, you should put out triangles or flares or anything including waving a flashlight or your arms to warn drivers to avoid colliding with an injured deer, or any other large animal. You should put your emergency flashers on to further alert other cars.

Construction

There are lower speed limits posted in construction zones because of changes of lanes, trucks pulling in and out of the area, workers who may be close to the lane of traffic, and barriers. It is important to obey these speed limits. Even if there are no workers present, frequently there are obstructions. The fines for speeding in construction zones are severe. Actually the majority of injuries and fatalities that occur are to drivers rather than workers, but the workers are in a very vulnerable situation. The use of cell phones is usually strictly prohibited in construction zones (as well as school zones).

SPECIAL WEATHER AND SEASONAL CONDITIONS

Rain

Early in a rain, oil and dirt (and in the Fall, leaves) on the surface can make the road very slippery. As you increase your speed in a heavy rain, you are more likely to hydroplane, i.e. you've lost your traction and you are basically gliding on the surface of the water. Gradually slow down until traction is again achieved. It is better not to hit the brakes hard but rather to take your foot off of the accelerator and if necessary very gently brake. Hydroplaning is a tricky and dangerous situation, and the faster you are going, the more likely you are to hydroplane. Avoidance of this situation is best. The more tread your tires have, the less likely you are to hydroplane.

Again, it is important to not use cruise control in the rain, or under other potentially slippery or dangerous conditions, since you will lose some of your own control of the vehicle. It is also the law in most states to have your headlights (not just running lights) on when your windshield wipers are on. This also applies to interval wipers. Speed should always be decreased.

It is also important to have reasonably fresh windshield wiper blades that can work effectively to clear the rain.

Snow

Snow presents many problems in terms of starting, driving stopping, and keeping good visibility. This is discussed in detail in the chapter on *winter driving*. For driving on ice or snow, it might be best to have even seven to eleven seconds between you and the vehicle in front of you. Most drivers will try to find roads that have recently been cleared.

Fog

In all the years I have been driving, fog is possibly the scariest and perhaps the most dangerous driving condition of all. It is especially important to both keep your distance from the car in front of you and still focus your attention on it. There is divided opinion regarding what to do if you have to pull over if you can't see at all. Some experts recommend getting out of the car and away from the road, and a number of other experts have stated that they feel that the car is the safest place because you have metal around you. This is a judgment call and it depends on the situation. If you can pull all the way to the right, off the road onto a shoulder, and safely and comfortably get out of the car, ideally on the passenger side, and get further away from the car and the road, I think that course of action is safer. You should turn your emergency flashers on to alert other drivers and you should turn your headlights off. If you are simply slowing down not intending to stop, tapping the brakes intermittently may give the signal to the driver behind you that you are slowing down without stopping.

The best advice is: **DON'T DRIVE IF FOG IS FORECAST OR ENCOUNTERED.**

As in most emergency situations, it is often best to ease off the accelerator and slow down rather than hitting the brakes or doing anything rapidly or suddenly. Your actual intention is to keep moving along slowly in traffic if possible.

> Use low beam headlights and avoid your high beam highway lights in a fog. If you have fog lights, and they are properly set, and they increase your ability to see, you can use them, with or without your regular low beam lights. Putting on your high beam lights causes the light to reflect back and impairs your vision.

I would again emphasize if you have to stop your car off the side of the road, that you should exit on the right side, away from traffic and get as far away from your car as possible, having put on your emergency flashers, and turning off your headlights.

Lightning

> Lightning will ordinarily be carried around the body of an all metal car into the ground. Therefore, as long as you are completely inside the car, you ordinarily cannot be harmed by lightning itself. It is best not to touch metal parts of the car, with either your feet or your hands if possible, of course assuming you are stopped. This relative protection is not necessarily true of a soft top convertible.

If lightning has struck a tree or if wind is blowing a tree down, there is a danger of injury or death if a tree falls onto and crushes your car. If it is lightning alone, as long as you are in a covered metal car, you are relatively safe. If it is windy and trees are coming down, or lightning is striking trees, then you have to be watchful. Getting away from a tree lined road, or stopping under an overpass could decrease danger from this cause.

If a live wire is touching your car, bus or truck, there is the possibility of explosion, fire or even electrocution. You should call for help. In some instances, you might be able to slowly and carefully drive out of the dangerous situation, but if the wire is live high voltage, any metal part of the car may be electrified and capable of electrocuting. If there is a downed live wire and there is water surrounding the car and if you get out of the car into a pool of water which is in contact with a downed live wire, you would likely be electrocuted. So, with a live wire in contact with your car, call 9-1-1 and wait for help. If there is a fire in the car and you have to leave the car in a lightning storm, with a live wire in contact with a puddle of water on the side of the car that you are jumping from, or connecting with a puddle on that side, you would have to jump from the car to a "dry spot," and you can't have one foot in the car and one foot on the ground. Your jump has to be such that both feet and any and all parts of your body leave the car before hitting the dry ground. There could be a situation where a wire was moving around, on the road, sparking, and/or your car was already on fire and you needed to move it to a dry spot so that you could safely escape the car. Even dry land can be electrified for up to 35 feet. Land with feet together, and take baby steps with feet close together for at least 35 feet.

Sunshine Delay

The sun shining in your eyes through the windshield or side window is usually most bothersome early in the morning and late in the afternoon, or early in the evening. It can be problematic, whether you are facing the sun or driving away from it, or at an angle where it is coming in through side windows. In any situation, it can be a distraction and sometimes even blinding. Sun visors help somewhat and there are items that you can purchase which can be attached to your sun visor which may be helpful, made of dark colored plastic. These may cause some minor distortion and be easily scratched. The sun may also reflect in your mirror or mirrors, necessitating shifting your seat position, or the mirror.

If you are caught in a situation where the sun is blinding, if you put up several fingers or even your hand between you and the sun, you may be able to partially block it out and see better. Squinting is also helpful, but difficult to do for long periods. Holding up a card or any opaque object may also work to some extent. Sunshine affecting your vision can clearly be a hazard in driving. It is one of the reasons that at certain times when the sun is in that position, it is a good idea to have your headlights on to help other drivers to be aware of your presence.

Sun glare can also occur at any time of the day and can come off of the windshield, the back window, the mirrors, the bumpers or fenders of another car, your car, even a building, and at times it can be blinding. It is often helpful to have sunglasses.

When your vision is being affected by the sun, keep a greater distance between you and the car in front of you and be watchful regarding staying in your lane. Although usually this situation is manageable, sometimes it is brutal and very dangerous. The sun sometimes will be shining almost directly behind cross traffic cars coming toward the intersection. You need to be patient and wait, and in some instances just simply turn into whichever direction you can see a clear path, and eventually get back to where you want to go.

Sun light can also make it difficult to see traffic signals, particularly if you are driving into the sun, and it is immediately behind or more often near the traffic light in your field of vision. Sometimes you will have to wait to see what other cars are doing in order to safely proceed or turn. Remember you can swivel your sun visor to block sun coming through the driver's window. The passenger side sun visor may also be helpful for sunlight coming in from that window's side or that side of the windshield.

Winter Driving

> Winter driving is basically a whole different ball game in many respects. There are two major conditions that affect winter driving, the first is cold weather, and the second is ice and snow.

In regards to cold weather, it is important to have sufficient emergency material onboard in case you are stalled in an area where help is not immediately available. Keep warm, it is suggested to use anything including newspapers, shopping bags, paper bags, even floor mats. This could include blankets and coats, food, water and cellular phones among other items. It is also important in cold weather, especially if you are traveling on the highway, to be certain that you keep your gas tank relatively full in case you encounter a traffic jam or you have a flat tire or some other problem. You want to have enough gas to get you through the situation. Although I would ordinarily recommend looking for a filling station when your gas tank reads half full, and making sure you fill it up when it is down to a quarter full, in extremely cold weather, especially on the highway, but even in the city if you are commuting, I would recommend filling your gas tank when it is down to half full, *or even sooner.* Experts say that cars with full gas tanks are less likely to freeze, especially overnight, another reason to keep your gas tank fuller in the winter.

> **It is important to remind drivers to not warm up a car in a garage, *even if the garage door is open*, since there is a great danger of carbon monoxide poisoning, both for the occupants of the car and of the house.**

Most feel that idling the car to warm it up is neither recommended nor necessary, rather it is best to just start out and drive slowly, gradually increasing your speed. A minute or two of idling doesn't seem to be excessively harmful, as long as it is outside the garage, and not close to air intakes or open windows. It is actually illegal in certain states to idle for more than a certain number of minutes.

> **Hybrids particularly are so quiet that they have occasionally been left with the motor running in a garage without the driver realizing it. In some tragic instances, the occupants of the houses affected died of carbon monoxide poisoning.**

Another aspect of cold weather driving is to be aware that pedestrians are bundled up and they are often wearing hats, gloves, and scarves, and their visual and hearing acuity may be lessened, so drivers have to be more alert.

Ice and Snow (See also Section on "Blizzards")

A good snow brush and ice scraper are essential items to be kept in every car in climates where snow and ice are possible.

> If your car is kept outside, and it has snowed heavily or even lightly, you need to clean your vehicle off thoroughly, paying particular attention to scraping ice or snow off of the windshield and rear window, front and rear lights, the license plates, the hood, the top, and also very importantly the side view mirrors, as well as all the windows.

One of the big problems in the winter with snow and ice is visibility, and drivers are tempted to scrape off some of the ice on the front windshield, turning on the defroster, and the rear window heater (defogger), and then to drive until the car warms up to the point where the heat clears the rest. Anything that interferes with your view can be dangerous and it is important to have all of these items completely clear before you start to drive.

> With snow or ice, it is very important to extend the interval between you and the car in front of you because your stopping distance will be greatly increased.

If you are going a relatively short distance and particularly if the road is icy, and if you are going at a slower speed, it might be a good idea to keep the car in a lower gear since you can also use the car's engine for additional braking, if necessary. If you are going fast and you suddenly down-shift on ice or snow, your car might skid.

An Anti-lock Braking System (ABS) is important to have. Even though you may not be able to stop more quickly with this, you will ordinarily maintain better control of the car. You will hear and feel the computer cutting in and out as it pumps the brakes and you **should keep pressure on the brake** and allow the computer to do its work. In a car without ABS, if the car skids, you should take your foot off the accelerator and gently pump the brake, short of locking up the wheels, and turn the steering wheel in the direction that the rear end has gone. **ABS is an important safety factor**. Its main purpose is to allow you to steer out of the situation without locking up any wheels, thereby helping to avoid losing control.

With slippery conditions such as snow and ice, be sure that you are depressing either the brake or the accelerator, **but not both at the same time.** The few people who drive with one foot on the brake and one foot on the accelerator may be doing this in rare instances to dry out excessively wet brakes from high standing water, but this is not recommended. Many cars are now equipped with brake interlocks (depressing the brake pedal shuts off the accelerator).

One of the keys to driving on ice and snow is the concept of GENTLE and GRADUAL in areas of BRAKING, ACCELERATING, and STEERING and it's best to not turn while braking or accelerating and turning at the same time, as well. While at times it might be necessary to both brake and turn at the same time, when you do both at the same time you are more likely to lose traction and to skid than if you did one at a time, and this applies to accelerating and turning at the same time as well.

With a rear wheel drive car, many experts advise putting 50 lbs. of sand or other weight in the rear trunk of the car, and sand has an advantage in that you can use that for traction under the tires if you are stuck on ice. Some would recommend an even greater amount of weight in a larger rear wheel drive car. You should be aware of whether your car is front wheel drive or rear wheel drive. Adding weight to the trunk of the car doesn't work on a front wheel drive car (may even lessen traction), and usually is not necessary in an all wheel drive or 4-wheel drive vehicle.

Try to keep a safe interval between you and the car in front, especially if you are behind a car or truck where snow is blowing off of it, because that can obstruct your view. If you haven't cleared off the top of your car and you have to stop suddenly, the snow and ice can slide down onto the front windshield and totally block your vision. If this is heavy and thick enough, it may not be able to be cleared by your windshield wipers.

Having good wiper blades and a windshield wiper fluid reservoir full of wiper fluid that will not freeze at usual winter temperatures is important during the winter.

When there is snow on the ground and the sidewalks are impassable, pedestrians may be walking in the street, sometimes on the right side of the road, instead of facing oncoming traffic. For this reason, be particularly careful because they could slip or wander into your path if you are not giving them enough space. If there is an early snow in the fall, and there are still piles of leaves in the street, this can cause an extra problem not only in terms of pedestrians, but even in terms of narrowing the street.

It is also important to wipe off the windshield wipers, especially removing ice from them. It is also necessary to clear the path for the windshield wiper fluid where it comes out, if this happens to be clogged or blocked by ice or snow.

On a rental car or unfamiliar car, be sure you know how to turn on the defroster quickly, if needed

Remember that the three elements in the winter that are important are visibility, traction, and driving style. The *driving style is smooth input at the steering wheel, accelerator, and brake.* Ideally when accelerating or braking you would not be turning at the same time.

For those parts of the country that generally have long lasting and heavy snows, "winter tires" have the advantage of more flexible rubber along with different tread. Although "all-season tires" may not work quite as well as winter tires in snow and ice, when paired with front wheel drive particularly, they seem to satisfy the needs of most drivers in many areas. If you do purchase winter tires, it is advised to change all four at the beginning of the winter and to remove them in the spring. If you only purchase two, it is advised to put them on the rear wheels, even in a front wheel drive car.

In the relatively flat Chicago area, most drivers do not change tires seasonally, in spite of often harsh, snowy and icy weather. In other areas, especially mountainous areas, particularly in northern latitudes, snow tires and chains are often standard equipment, and some states will allow studded snow tires, at least through the winter.

With slippery conditions, brake gradually before you go into a turn and steer through the turn or corner at a safe speed. This is particularly true on ice. On regular dry pavement you can sometimes accelerate slightly as you go through a curve, assuming that you've slowed down to a safe speed before you entered the curve.

In the winter, anticipate that you may need extra time to clear the car of ice and snow or frost in the morning, especially when you are getting ready to go to work, if you keep your car or cars outdoors. Since there can often be unsuspected snow or cold weather during the night, it is generally a good idea to check weather reports and if snow or ice is predicted, get up a little earlier to allow for the extra time possibly needed. When you get up in the morning, first look outside to see if there is snow or ice on your car. Under adverse weather conditions, even if you have cleared snow and ice from your car, other cars may not have adequately cleared their windows as well, and having your headlights on (and not just your daytime running lights) will aid other cars in knowing your position, thus decreasing the likelihood of an accident.

On snow or ice, your vehicle traction is only 1/2 to 1/4 as great as you are accustomed to on dry pavement. If you sense wheel spin, ease up on the gas pedal and try to gradually get the tires to grip again.

> **With heavy snows in the winter, often there are huge piles of snow at the edge of parking lots or driveways, not only making parking difficult, but also making it difficult to see cars exiting from parking lots, driveways and intersections. Both the car that may have to stop, approaching the intersection, as well as the car that might have the right of way, should be cautious remembering that visibility can be greatly decreased because of this.**

Heavy snow can obscure driveway entrances,
and cars entering intersections.

Driving, as always, is a full time job and particularly in the winter with adverse weather conditions, distractions should be avoided.

> **In blowing snow, stop signs and traffic lights can be obliterated, which creates significant additional hazards. Cross traffic may not be aware of obliterated stop signs or traffic lights. Often other signs along the road which indicate exits or entrances or special conditions such as construction, can also be obliterated as well. Much more caution is needed under those circumstances.**

Try to avoid splashing pedestrians if there is slush or even puddles of water after melting of snow, or after a heavy rain.

> **Watch out for bridges, exit and entrance ramps, and overpasses and anywhere else where ice may form under conditions where other areas may be free of ice.**

If you get stuck in deep snow or an icy spot, or in a freezing rain, it is recommended you use salt or kitty litter under and in front and behind the drive wheels. Sand may also help, as can carpet remnants, and there are certain pads that can be purchased that are specifically useful for that purpose. Even car mats may be helpful. It may also help to start out in second gear rather than first gear. You can also use a lower gear to help when braking if you are not going too fast. So you up-shift to start and you down-shift to stop, or if just going a short distance, you can just keep it in second gear for slower and shorter trips to use your engine to help with braking on ice and/or snow. This will probably be done less often with an automatic transmission. Down-shifting at higher speeds should be done in stages.

If you park your car outside, try to place the front windshield facing the rising sun. That may make it easier to clean frost, ice and snow off of your car in the morning. You can put on the rear defroster and that will often start melting ice and snow as you are clearing the other windows and the rest of the car.

If you live in a particularly harsh climate, in fact probably most of the United States, consider keeping a small shovel in the trunk to remove excess ice and snow from around the tires in the event that you become stuck.

> **Be particularly careful in cold weather not to leave pets, elderly passengers, or children in unattended cars.**

The term black ice refers to a coating of clear (transparent) ice, over usually a black roadway, making it more difficult to spot. It can occur with rain or even fog at the right temperature or with shady icy areas in the winter. You can encounter black ice on level roads as well as hilly or mountainous roads, particularly if in the shade. Control is usually lost, and braking will not help. Awareness and going slowly with caution are advised. Sometimes cautiously testing your braking ability when there are no cars or traffic around is helpful.

Summer Driving

> **Remember that a locked car with the windows closed during the summer can quickly attain a temperature of over 120 degrees. This can be fatal to pets, children, and even adults, especially elderly adults. Door handles, steering wheels, metal parts of seat belts and their latches, and even seats can become intolerably and dangerously hot.**

If you are driving in the summer and you notice that your car is overheating, you may have a broken fan belt, in which case you may soon see smoke coming out from under the hood. If you are low on coolant or just overtaxing the cooling system, a very temporary measure which might help you to get to the next maintenance station or mechanic, is to turn off the air conditioner.

Be certain coolant level and windshield cleaning fluid levels are adequate.

Pollen from trees, bushes, and weeds, blocking visibility through windows and windshields, and bugs splattering on the windshield are just some of summer's driving problems. Overgrown shrubbery and trees blocking visibility of street signs, stop signs, sidewalks, and even traffic lights, are more likely to occur in the spring and summer.

Trees can obscure a stop sign until you are very close to it.

Hay fever or other seasonal allergic conditions may be more bothersome in the Spring, Summer and Fall, causing sneezing, runny nose, coughing, or blurry and teary eyes.

Expect to encounter more bicyclists during the warmer months, especially kids on bikes, scooters, and rollerblades, during summer vacation, and also expect to encounter more motorcycles during the warmer months.

Fall Driving

Leaves, either on the car or more likely in the street, often in large piles, are often a problem in terms of residential areas and parking. It is possible, if you park your car on a pile of dried leaves, that this could cause the leaves to catch on fire, although this is unlikely. Leaves can also be slippery. Sometimes, when there are large piles of leaves on the sidewalk, pedestrians might choose to walk in the street. There can be overgrown bushes and trees that can obscure signs in the Fall as well as in the Spring and Summer.

Leaves in the street can take up parking
spaces and narrow the street.

In late Fall, depending upon where you live, snow can be an issue as can cold weather and ice.

ROAD RAGE

ROAD RAGE HAS BECOME INCREASINGLY COMMON in recent years, and the results have been much more serious, often tragic. Road rage basically means that you the driver may have had your emotions controlled by the other driver, or vice versa. At that point, if you are an unwilling or willing participant, you overreact and it becomes a contest that frequently ends in a violent and sometimes fatal confrontation. Part of this section utilizes the excellent format found in the 2009 and 2013 Aggressive Driving Section of the State of Illinois Rules of the Road. Reproduction is with permission from the Office of Jesse White, Illinois Secretary of State.

To avoid road rage on the part of another driver, you need to avoid aggressive driving. This means not doing anything that endangers or is likely to endanger persons or property, or upsets other drivers. This could include any of the following:

- Making eye contact with other drivers who have done something that you interpret as aggressive and upsetting to you, and this may include facial gestures, or improper hand gestures, either by you or other drivers, or even passengers
- Honking the horn repeatedly and usually without justification
- Cutting off another vehicle
- Turning right on red in front of a cross traffic vehicle (this is a form of cutting off another vehicle)
- Running red lights and/or stop signs
- Tailgating (an extremely serious and dangerous action that often causes crashes)
- Speeding (usually speeding endangers the speeder and others around him or her, but in my opinion, probably is not as much a cause of road rage as some of the other actions)

- Passing on the shoulder of the road
- Slamming on the brakes in front of someone who is tailgating you, i.e. trying to "teach the tailgater a lesson," (this does not refer to appropriate and safe stopping for a yellow or red light)
- Repeated vocal contact which generally is yelling, frequently using offensive language
- Failing to dim high beam headlights, especially if it blinds the driver in the car ahead of you, or if you flash headlights just as an opposing car is about to pass you, which is not only totally improper, but dangerous as well; Flashing lights to warn oncoming drivers of dangers should be far enough away (500 feet) so as not to blind them.

Your response to an aggressive or angry driver should be the following:

- Remain calm and do not take it personally. The other driver may be incompetent, may have a true emergency, or may have simply made a mistake.
- Do not retaliate or try to get even in any way.
- Try to remove yourself from the confrontation by pulling over into another lane, or even pulling off the road if necessary.
- Avoid eye contact.
- Lock your doors and keep your windows rolled up.
- Keep enough space between you and a stopped vehicle in front of you to be able to pull around the vehicle, if necessary.

Be aware that an angry or aggressive driver may be mentally unbalanced, and even armed. It is never worth it to get involved in a contest where there is no winner. A mature driver will simply let it pass and try to keep from escalating the confrontation.

Additionally, other things that you can do which will help you to avoid becoming an aggressive driver, or the victim of an aggressive driver's road rage:

- Avoid conflicts, even if you are in the right.
- Allow extra time to get to your destination so that you are not rushing and "pushing the envelope."

- Do not drive when overtired or upset, or angry.
- Try to pick less congested roads or less busy times of the day to travel.
- Again, be forgiving of the other driver, i.e. give them the benefit of the doubt since what they have done may be out of lack of driving skill, and/or may have been completely unintentional. Even if you know that it was intentional, just forget it.
- In the end, be patient and courteous.

If, in spite of doing everything you can to avoid becoming involved in a road rage incident, you nevertheless are involved, call 9-1-1, give your location and the description of your car and the other car. If you have stopped, which in itself is often a bad idea, keep your windows up and your doors locked. If the other motorist comes out of the car with a weapon, or is otherwise threatening, then you could pull away from or around the driver, and drive to a police station, a busy filling station or other location that may discourage the raging driver from further action. Keep the police informed of your intention and location and use your flashers and if necessary honk your horn to gain attention. Ask the 9-1-1 operator to stay on the phone until police arrive.

Remember that many drivers are immigrants, tourists, elderly, or at least older drivers, and some are young inexperienced drivers. It is important to remember that there is a real variety of drivers with a wide range of actual ability and commitment to responsible driving.

The safe, courteous, and responsible driver will show maturity and will ignore the bad, inconsiderate and rude driver. If they encounter a driver who is clearly posing a danger, they will try to get their license number and vehicle description to phone it into the proper authorities.

Honking aggressively, especially unnecessarily, is particularly important to avoid since this has a significant potential for irritating other drivers. Serious tailgating may be in the same category.

Driving too slowly is occasionally another potential instigator of road rage. If you can't drive at a reasonable legal speed on a highway, freeway, expressway or tollway, then you should consider taking an alternate route.

To me, the right attitude as a driver is to not feel that everybody is out to irritate or inconvenience or endanger you, but rather that driving is difficult, and some drivers are not that familiar with the road, or do not have good driving habits or even skills. If a driver needs to get into your lane at a certain spot, be courteous and let him or her in. Put yourself in their position, where they may be unfamiliar with the roadway and the circumstances, and try to be courteous.

> **In terms of not taking anything personally, remember that someone who honks at you or cuts in front of you, most likely doesn't even know who you are, so it very likely is *not* personal.**

It is also important to avoid getting into arguments over parking spaces because those arguments can quickly become heated, violent and even deadly. Try to use patience more than your horn. Also use judgment, and have an escape route.

An aggressive driver might be on drugs or might be impaired or otherwise represent a danger to themselves and to you. So just cool it and drive defensively. Take care of yourself and try not to ever get into a road rage encounter.

Don't honk your horn at someone unless you might be saving their life or avoiding an accident by alerting them. Spouses, as well as other passengers, have every right to complain of bad driving habits or displays of temper.

There is some evidence that road rage is learned in childhood, perhaps by observing parents or other adults exhibiting that. It is very important for parents to set a proper example for their children.

> **SUMMARY: Road rage can be initiated by actions of a driver, and road rage can also be the result of an over-response of a driver. There is no real way to summarize since all the points in this chapter are extremely important and my strong recommendation is that it be read and understood in its entirety.**

USE OF YOUR HORN

USE YOUR BRAKES MORE THAN YOUR **horn to avoid accidents.** Sometimes you might have to use both, but probably the brakes should ordinarily come first. If you fail to use your horn when it was appropriate to avoid an accident, you could be judged to be the cause of the accident, or at least not utilizing a means of avoiding an accident, which might be considered the same.

If the car in the lane next to you seems to be coming over the line into your lane and you think the person is not paying attention, or might be impaired or even falling asleep, use your brake first, and then your horn if necessary and appropriate. If you decide that you do need to pass that car, then a little beep, or in some instances a big honk, seems to be appropriate as long as it is judiciously used to avoid an accident, and not merely aggressively. It may be useful to startle a drowsy driver into alertness temporarily, and give them a chance to find a rest spot.

If an *approaching car* is crossing the centerline and coming into your lane and you likely won't be able to avoid it by braking, then most drivers would honk loudly, but at the same time they should be pulling to the right and trying to get off the road. You may be able to gradually brake at that point. It is definitely advised to not try to go left into the lane the drifting car has vacated, because they might suddenly recognize what they've done and try to recover, and that would cause a head on collision. It is also advised not to necessarily come to a complete stop, since your ability to avoid a collision might be diminished by stopping, rather than pulling safely as far to the right as you can.

"Fixation" as explained to me by my friend, Burton Siegal, refers to a tendency in an emergency for a driver to aim the car to where the driver is looking, and for that reason, if you are faced with an impending collision, you should be looking at your escape route, and not at the car headed toward you.

> **If you are behind a car when the light changes and you can see that the driver is looking down at something or off to the side and not paying attention, after several seconds, it seems reasonable to give a slight beep, but don't lean on the horn. Usually a slight beep to timely help them be aware that the light has changed would ordinarily be appreciated, and they would not likely take offense.**

If you are backing up and you hear a horn, stop immediately. It might be someone who is trying to avoid an accident, or it might be someone trying to alert you of a problem with your car. So check your instrument panel to be sure none of the trouble lights are on, including if there is a loss of tire air pressure, which can be indicated on the instrument panel in newer cars.

If you are changing lanes and you hear a horn, then check to see if you have miscalculated the opening in the lane next to you, and if it is necessary to rethink your move.

If a car in front of you has backed up from the intersection because of a red light and they didn't change to a forward gear after backing up, when they start up again when the light changes, they might go backwards instead of forwards, so you might want to honk before or as the light changes, in that situation.

It is especially improper if a driver is trying to be cautious getting through a tight intersection or other traffic situation, and you are right behind them blaring on the horn. Don't use your horn to express frustration or other emotions. Unnecessarily leaning on the horn is one of the surest ways to incur road rage and should clearly be avoided. Honk appropriately when you need to, and avoid honking when it isn't necessary or appropriate.

BACKING UP

MANY DRIVING INSTRUCTORS SAY THAT YOU should be able to turn all the way around and look out the back window while backing up. That's uncomfortable for some, and even then it is difficult to see on your left if you are turning to the right as most do. I have found that monitoring all three mirrors in sequence and looking out the back window and *going very slowly* is my preferred way of backing up. When backing up into a street, do not cross the center line, unless you are intending to go in that direction. Make sure that the road is clear in both directions.

Many, and eventually all, newer model cars will have back-up cameras which give you a view on the dash as long as the car is in reverse, although bright sunlight renders some of them difficult to view. Some newer cars have vastly improved the view and color, and some have grid lines to help you judge distance. These newer cameras are often less affected by sunlight. Many trucks have loud beeps that have nothing to do with detecting objects behind them and are meant to alert pedestrians and other drivers that the trucks are backing up. Some cars have beeping to warn of an obstacle while backing up, but by the late teens of this century, most or all cars will have cameras.

When vision is impaired by parked vans, SUVs, or trucks, and in most other situations it is much better to back up a few inches at first, and then, if clear, possibly eight or nine inches, and at some point, you'll be in a position to see on either side. A very important part of this section of advice is to make certain that there are no children playing behind you when you back up, particularly in a driveway or parking lot. Watch for small children, pets and toys, as well as pedestrians. Backing up very slowly in a parking lot also makes it less likely that you will be hit by cars driving by, often going much faster than is appropriate for a parking lot. Rear cross-traffic alert is becoming available.

TEENAGE (AND OTHER BEGINNING) DRIVERS

TEENAGERS, PARTICULARLY THOSE WHO ARE BEGINNING drivers, have more accidents than other age groups, partly because the area of the brain that is involved in risk assessment and judgment has not yet developed. Scientists have shown that this area usually doesn't develop until age 21. We've all known exceptions on either side. Nevertheless, on average, teenagers are more likely to be involved in accidents, including fatal accidents. They are also more likely to be at fault in their crashes, and their violations are more likely to be single vehicle fatal accidents.

One suggestion I offer is that driver education should start when children are old enough to see outside of the car, and to understand what is being discussed. In other words, as parents drive safely, with courtesy and responsibility, they should explain certain select circumstances, and reasons for their action in response to a situation, to their children. Even children who are not yet at an age where they can intelligently discuss this are still influenced by the examples that their parents can set.

There are Graduated Licensing Laws (GLL) enacted by many, if not most, states (differing slightly from state to state) and it important to obtain the driver's license manual (often called by other names) from the state in which you are licensed, to be aware of the details. The law generally increases the time that a permit is held, i.e. learning before an examination and a license is granted, and they mandate a certain number of hours, often fifty behind the wheel with an adult, usually ten of these hours required to be at night. Some high school driver education classes offer some supervised behind the wheel driving and also a certain number of classroom hours. If a private driving school is considered, proof of certification of the school should be requested and provided. In spite of all the extra supervision and training, driving or driving alone may still be a scary experience for a 16 year old. A parent needs to know the strong and weak points of their teenaged beginning (new) driver. Alcohol, certain medications, and recreational drugs should be totally out of the question. Passengers, especially teenagers, should be limited until a fair amount of experience has been gained.

Once a youngster is over 12, they may be in the front seat with their father or mother, or other experienced driver, and this type of teaching could be invaluable, regardless of whether the youngster is in the front seat or the back seat.

It should be noted that the rear seat is still safer than the front passenger seat, and this may be especially true in light of all of the airbag recalls. Toyota has indicated that if a car needs a recall for a passenger side airbag, if they are not yet available, the passenger should be seated in the back seat rather than the front passenger seat. One Acura dealer strongly advised the same. It may turn out that all of the airbags, especially if made by Takata, may pose a danger, in Toyota and possibly in many other makes of cars.

There are standardized forms for contracts which are recommended between parents and their teenage drivers, and these are available through AAA and other resources, including many state's Department of Transportation (DOT).

For the young driver, as for all drivers, it is important to have the proper insurance documents (usually a card) in the car, and if traveling out of state, the registration of the vehicle. The driver must always have their driver's license with them.

Tape an index card or a sheet of paper inside the glove box, and indicate the persons and their phone numbers that your son or daughter may have to call, or your spouse or parents, and what to say and present to a police officer or other authority in case of an accident or traffic stop.

It is the parent's job to make sure that their children know how to handle a vehicle in most every circumstance, by riding with them and supervising what they do. While some of this may partially be the responsibility of a driving school, ultimately the parents are responsible for their children and they need to be assured that they do have the proper skill and judgment.

Show your teenagers how to do a walk-around the car with each lesson before getting into the car. Ask them to try to spot anything unusual, particularly involving the windows, tires, and obstacles at the front or back of the car, including children, pets, or other vehicles, and also importantly make sure the mirrors are properly adjusted. **Checking the tire pressure on a monthly basis is very important and remember that when you can actually see that a tire is low, it has already lost over half of its pressure.**

> **It is especially important that teenagers do have a cell phone to call for help in an emergency. They should not be called, and they should not initiate or receive other than emergency calls while they are driving, and then they should pull into a parking space or parking lot to retrieve or initiate a cellular phone call or a response.**

There are a number of books that are designed for parents who have the time and inclination to work with their teenager or other beginning driver in terms of progressively learning how to drive. This might be especially useful when high school driver's education classes are unavailable, or may even be useful when they are. There are probably many parents who won't have the time to be able to do this in this much detail, but for those who can and wish to, the following books are recommended: "Safe Young Drivers, A Guide for Parents and Teens" by Phil Berardelli, published by Mountain Lake Press, Mountain Lake Park, Maryland; "Crash-Proof Your Kids (Make your Teen a Safer, Smarter Driver)" by Timothy C. Smith, published by Simon and Schuster. These books may also be available through Amazon.com.

Parents of a teenager beginning to drive should also read the chapter in this book on the choice of a safe car.

Good reference websites are the National Highway Transportation Safety Administration (NHTSA), SaferCars.gov and the Insurance Institute for Highway Safety (IIHS). Edmunds.com, and also Consumer Reports are good resources for choosing a car that is safe. The recommended cars can change from year to year. You need to know your youngster well enough to know whether to provide a possibly under powered 4-cylinder car, or possibly an over powered 6-cylinder car with advantages and disadvantages of both. Many of the newer 4-cylinder cars are very peppy, but with multiple passengers, air conditioning, etc. this peppiness may be decreased in some cars.

In Chicago and the entire state of Illinois, great credit goes to the Illinois Secretary of State Jesse White, and the *Chicago Tribune* for running a detailed series on teenage accidents, particularly fatalities, which led to the graduated licensing laws in Illinois.

Teenage drivers need to be aware of the curfew hours, which can differ from village to village, and from city to city, and also on week days versus weekends (Friday evening, Saturday and Sunday).

Speed is often a factor in many teen crashes. During a teenager's first 500 miles of driving, they are much more likely to crash than an adult. Two thirds of the teenagers who died in car accidents were not buckled up. Since crash rates are much higher in teenagers, it is necessary to emphasize how important it is for them to especially pay close attention, drive responsibly, drive safely, and drive without distraction.

Weekends and nighttime or adverse conditions such as rain or snow seem to be more problematic for teenagers. The hours just before and just after school are particularly risky for teen drivers, and speed is again one of the leading factors in teen driving fatalities. Distractions and alcohol are also very important causes or contributions to crashes.

Some teenagers tend to take more risks. It is important for all drivers to be especially respectful of a car that has a sign on top or elsewhere saying that they are a driving school, since it might be an inexperienced student driver who might make an unexpected move. Generally speaking, those situations are well controlled by the instructors, and they are very unlikely to cause or be involved in an accident. A beginning driver with a permit or even a license may have a magnetic strip on the trunk or bumper indicating their status. Give them extra space, and also extra patience.

Carnegie Mellon University Professor Paul Fishback has shown that a high risk taking teenager and an older woman in the 80s, as drivers, present about the same risk. With education and acceptance of responsibility, both groups can significantly decrease their risks.

Teenagers driving alone tend to take the same risks as adults, but when in the car with other young people, they tend to run more red lights. Having young people in the car seems to be a consistent risk factor, and the more young people there are in the car, the greater the risk factor. Graduated licensing laws in most states will clearly delineate how many passengers are allowed at different phases of licensing, and may further limit the number of non-family passengers during the early phases of driving.

Unsafe turns are probably among the most common cause of accidents in teenage drivers. Allow yourself enough time and be cautious and patient. Automobile accidents are actually the number one killer of teenagers in America. The first 500 miles are the most dangerous.

To repeat, the most common mistakes made by an inexperienced driver, especially a teenage driver, are:

① speeding
② over-crowding the car
③ not wearing a seat belt
④ being distracted, especially by other passengers
⑤ consuming alcohol or legal or illegal drugs, including marijuana.

The order of importance is not necessarily as listed and all are significant.

Young drivers ideally should not listen to loud music, in fact it is often best not to listen to anything, with the exception of traffic and adverse weather reports. It is usually better to just concentrate on the road.

> **There are multiple limitations and requirements that apply to beginning drivers and it is important for the teenage drivers and their parents to review the rules of the road and these restrictions and limitations carefully, and to understand them fully.**

According to Robert Duffer, of the *Chicago Tribune* (The Rides section August 28, 2016), Chevrolet, on many of its models, addresses parent's concerns over teen driving. The so-called "teen driver" provides an alert and a report card indicating how the teen drove, including distance traveled, extreme braking, even tailgating alerts and speeding, and has other safety features. Mr. Duffer comments that while other automakers have teen monitoring systems, Chevy seems to be the most comprehensive.

SENIOR DRIVERS

I T IS A GOOD IDEA TO talk to an older driver before issues arise, acknowledging how difficult the topic can be, along with offers for emotional support, and mentioning the driver refresher courses they could take. Adaptive equipment might make a difference, and also seniors taking medication in the afternoon could make them drowsy, and they might agree to drive only in the morning. They should discuss that with their doctor. Respect their desire to make their own decisions.

Older drivers are often very capable, but they may experience a lessening of physical, and in some instances, mental capabilities. They may lose some flexibility, mobility, and strength, and also visual acuity, making it more difficult to adjust to the speed of traffic, and to read road signs. Senior drivers may have difficulty with different types of lighting, especially low light, or glare from headlights and overhead lights at night.

With older drivers, bones may become more brittle and this means that an older driver is more likely to be severely, even fatally, injured in an accident.

If a senior has trouble with steering, they could try using a turning knob. Keep a safe distance behind the car in front of you as mentioned in other parts of this book, i.e. the three or four second rule, which can be much greater depending upon weather, road and traffic conditions, and even the driver's own condition. Try to maintain good flexibility and mobility so that you can look through the rear window and the mirrors when you are backing up. When changing lanes look out the left or right front and rear windows after checking your rear view and your side view mirror, and of course signal your intent.

Older drivers often have their vision particularly affected by cataracts, glaucoma, and macular degeneration, and they should have a yearly examination by a competent eye doctor. Headlights, as well as mirrors and windows, should be kept clean and scratch free, and even the driver's eyeglasses should be kept clean and free of scratches.

If a driver has lost some peripheral vision, they may need to turn their head frequently to compensate for this. Some suggest avoiding wearing eyeglasses and sun glasses with wide frames or temples that may restrict their side vision. Use a cushion or pillow if needed to comfortably see over the steering wheel, and make sure that you can comfortably reach the gas pedal and brake pedal.

Hearing often decreases somewhat as we get older. The sound of horns, motorcycles, sirens or even screeching tires and revving motors can warn you of hazards. One sign that you may be having trouble hearing is if you don't hear horns or sirens when the car windows are rolled up. Another criterion could be whether or not you hear the sound of your turn signals when they are on. The loudness can differ from car to car. Because of a decrease in hearing, it is important to look at the mirrors for emergency vehicles, and if possible, keep the window slightly open or even more so in the warmer weather, and keep the radio off or turned down so that you will be able to hear the sirens of emergency vehicles.

Some older drivers will have a decrease in cognition which will affect perception, reasoning, judgment, intuition, and even memory. Reaction time often increases and reflexes may become slower as we age.

Older drivers are more likely to have medical conditions which may interfere with safe driving, such as seizure disorders, episodes of dizziness, sleep disorders, lapse of concentration, or even loss of consciousness. Parkinson's Disease, stroke, and vertigo, as well as heart attacks, arthritis, diabetes, and some other medical conditions, are more likely to occur in older drivers than in younger ones.

Since alcohol impairs judgment and distorts decision making, and also hinders coordination, as well as slowing reflexes, it is especially important that older drivers not drink and drive. This is important at all ages. Marijuana should not be mixed with driving.

Sometimes restrictions are placed on older drivers, such as to not drive during rush hour traffic, at night, or being allowed to drive only to their physician, grocery, house of worship, and selected other important destinations.

If you wear glasses, bring your most recent prescription to your driving test, but ask your eye doctor if you should wear them for your vision test, and your driving test. This is especially true if your glasses are only for near (close vision), or if you use bifocals. In Illinois you can also see an eye care professional to verify your visual acuity and thereby bypass your vision exam up to several months before your license renewal date.

Signs that may indicate an unsafe driver include the following:

- dents and scrapes, not only on the car, but also on garage doors, fences, mailboxes, light poles, etc.
- drifting across lane markers or into other lanes
- ignoring or missing signs and traffic signals
- driving too slowly or too fast (especially driving slowly in a passing lane)
- getting lost in places that are otherwise familiar
- frequent accidents, or even close calls
- delay in, or late, braking
- difficulty judging openings in traffic (**particularly hazardous with left turns)**
- being often honked at by other drivers
- finding that relatives and friends are reluctant to drive with them
- having a difficult time concentrating or being easily distracted while driving
- difficulty turning their head to check over their shoulder when backing up,
- difficulty looking out the windows when changing lanes
- receiving frequent warnings or traffic tickets from police officers
- having difficulty finding their parked vehicle, something that can be difficult in some venues at any age, perhaps especially at sports or other facilities that are completely surrounded by parking
- difficulty reading traffic signs
- not using turn signals,
- not canceling turn signals when used for half turns or expressway entrances and exits
- stopping inappropriately, such as for green lights, or in the middle of an intersection when not turning

- pulling out from a parking space without checking traffic
- lack of awareness of pedestrians, motorcyclists or bicyclists,
- cars, or people walking, which seem to appear out of nowhere

Many older drivers will choose to not drive at night, and they will only drive during daytime when traffic is light. They may not only avoid difficult intersections, but they may choose to turn right three times rather than turning left. If they are unable to comfortably drive on expressways at the usual indicated speed limit (not the minimum speed limit), they could use alternate routes.

Older drivers are likely to be on more medications, both prescription and non-prescription, than younger drivers. They should always check with their physician and/or pharmacist regarding the possible effect on operating dangerous machinery while taking their medications. In almost all instances, it is better to establish how a medication affects them over a period of several days before even attempting to drive, especially if there is that type of caution on the label or from their professional.

Older (and all) drivers should be certain that they are at least 10 (preferably 12) inches away from the steering wheel to prevent excessive injury or even death in the event the air bag deploys in a crash, or even without a crash. The airbag should not be aimed at the neck, face, or head. Use seat cushions and pedal extenders if necessary.

There are driver rehabilitation specialists who can sometimes help to evaluate and correct problems that older drivers might have. These are generally occupational therapists or other professionals who are specially trained. They can usually be found in the occupational therapy department of a local hospital.

Many older drivers, becoming aware of changes in their body and mind, can refocus their attention and continue to drive safely, albeit sometimes under restricted conditions. Studies have shown that while older drivers may take longer to react, their decision or response is usually wiser and safer.

If an older driver, or for that matter a driver at any age, has dementia or cognitive problems, the family and the driver need to work with a medical team to decide if driving is still safe, and the Department of Motor Vehicle licensing would also be involved at some point. In some instances, for the sake of the driver and the motoring and pedestrian public safety, they may need to stop driving.

For those who do have to quit driving, friends and family may help out, there may be delivery services, taxi's, public transportation and other means of getting around. They can find out about services in their area by contacting www.eldercare.gov or 1-800-677-1116, and their state department of transportation.

ROADWAY SIGNS

THE READER IS STRONGLY ENCOURAGED TO refer to the driving manual of their state, or Rules of the Road. While I have permission from the Office of Jesse White, the Illinois Secretary of State, to use the organization and content of this and other sections of the 2009 and 2013 State of Illinois "Rules of the Road," what I chose to present in this book is a much briefer condensation of that section, perhaps directed more toward safety considerations. **I would urge every driver to review their state driver's manual and to obtain the yearly revisions of the Rules of the Road, since the rules and laws and regulations may change from year to year**.

The eight- sided red sign usually with white letters saying STOP, always indicates a complete stop at the stop line. There is often a thin white border around the entire Stop sign. Sometimes there is a border of small flashing lights to also enhance attention. If there is no stop line, stop before entering the crosswalk. If there is no crosswalk, stop before entering the intersection.

A three- sided sign, which usually is white in the center, the outer half or third being red, **basically a triangle pointing *downward*, states and means *Yield* the right of way. You must let all traffic and pedestrians near you go before you proceed, i.e. give them the right of way. Slow down to a safe speed and *STOP* if necessary.** This is discussed in detail elsewhere in this book. *Yield* signs are often posted where the entrance lane is not long enough to permit drivers to speed up sufficiently to safely *merge* with main roads or highways after exiting a freeway or expressway or other traffic.

A round yellow sign means railroad crossing ahead and those require much attention and caution. They often have a large black X and the letters RR. It is important, if necessary, to roll down your vehicle windows and listen to make certain other noises do not block out the sound of a train. If there is any chance that a train is approaching, stop and wait. **Unfortunately, there have been tragic train/vehicle accidents when signals and gates were inoperative. Cross railroad tracks only if there is definitely adequate space for your vehicle on the other side of the tracks. See the section in this book on Railroad Crossings.**

Diamond shaped signs mean "Warning." These signs warn you about hazards or possible hazards on or near the roadway, and you should slow down and use caution.

For the sake of brevity, I would just mention that you should become familiar with the following signs by looking at your state driver's manual in regards to the following:

A **No Passing Zone** sign; an **All Way Stop** sign; **Do Not Enter** sign; **Wrong Way** sign; **Not Allowed** sign; **One Way** sign; **Two Way Left Turn Lane** sign; **No Turn On Red** sign; **Divided Highway** sign; **Keep Right** sign; **Do Not Pass** sign; **Pass With Care** sign (these will tell you that you are at the end of the no passing zone and you may now pass, but **only when and if it is safe**); **School Zone** warning sign; **Stop Ahead / Yield Ahead / Signal Ahead** sign; **Intersection Ahead** sign; **Turns and Curve signs** (be aware that maximum safe speed is exactly what it says, maximum under ideal circumstances, such as a dry road and good light. Under certain circumstances that speed should definitely be less then the posted speed.); **Exit Ramp** sign (This also show a maximum safe speed a vehicle can be driven on the ramp. This can be modified greatly by road or weather conditions, as well as time of day and traffic.); **Slippery Pavement** sign (shows a car with squiggly lines behind both back tires and this warns that especially the particular road can be slippery and dangerous when wet); **A Downgrade** sign (It is a good idea to shift to allow your motor to assist in braking. Some signs will indicate that this needs to be done.); **Narrow Bridge** sign (warns of an upcoming bridge that may not be wide enough for two cars to pass in opposite directions at the same time); **Reduction in Lanes** sign (indicates that lanes going in the same direction may be merging into fewer lanes); **Merging Lanes** sign (**The driver on the expressway should be far enough behind the vehicle in front to provide space for a merging car. Drivers on the entrance ramp should be aware that they can pick up speed on the approach lane so that they can more easily and successfully merge.**);

Stop and Go signal lights (these are often placed before entrance ramps at busy sites to separate the cars that are entering during peak traffic hours, to avoid excess congestion of merging traffic.); **Two Way Roadway** sign (with arrows going in both directions, i.e. up and down, tells the driver that they are leaving a divided roadway and will be driving on a two-lane, two-way road.); **Construction and Maintenance Signs** (Every year, work zone traffic crashes account for thousands of injuries and many fatalities, especially to motorists, but also to construction workers. Use extreme caution when entering areas where workers and/or slow moving vehicles and/or barricades are present, even if work is not going on at the time. A driver must always obey the posted work zone speed limit. This could be because of the presence of workers, or even in the absence of workers, since normal driving conditions do not exist in a work zone. There may be narrow lanes, drop offs between lanes or at the edge of pavement, lane closures, or construction equipment or obstructions near open lanes of traffic.);

The use of wireless communication devices is prohibited in Illinois while driving in a construction or maintenance speed zone.

Barricades and vertical panels; **Warning Lights and Arrow Boards**; **Signs indicating a Flag Person**; **Photo Speed Enforcement** signs; **Slow Moving Vehicle** signs; **Mile posts (one type of Guide Sign** placed every mile along the highway from one end of the state to the other, **Zero usually starts at the south and west borders of the state.** These mile posts may also be useful in reporting emergencies to authorities in case of an accident or other situation requiring assistance. With GPS so widely available, this is probably of less significance.); **Red Light Camera** signs; **Signs** indicating reduced speed in school and park zones.

This is a very condensed version of what appears in the Rules of the Road of the State of Illinois, reproduced with the permission of the office of Jesse White, Illinois Secretary of State. Many of the items in each years' "Rules of the Road" could change at any time in the future, and the laws and regulations pertaining to them could also change. Every driver is encouraged to review their own state's Rules of the Road on a yearly basis and you are particularly encouraged to look at the more complete description and pictures of the various signs and the actions that are required because of these signs.

PASSENGERS

If you are a passenger in an automobile, you have every right to express your opinion about the way the car is being driven. This is true even if the driver is a relative or close friend, or a taxi cab driver. You can be tactful and say, "I'm uncomfortable with the speed with which you are driving," or "I'm uncomfortable in regards to safety and the way you are driving." This is true if the driver is going through stop signs, running red lights, speeding, not keeping his or her hands on the wheel, being unduly distracted, or being guilty of any other infraction. The driver does have a responsibility of transporting all of his or her passengers and himself or herself to the selected destination, safely and comfortably.

You can assist if you are a passenger in the front seat in terms of changing radio stations or bands, handling CDs, or other media, making phone calls, including emergency phone calls, adjusting the heater, air conditioning, defroster and the rear window defroster, inputting into the GPS if necessary, navigating maps, and reading road signs. In other words, anything that you can do as a passenger that will help the driver to keep focusing on driving is appropriate. You should tell the driver that you'd be happy to do that if the driver doesn't ask you to.

P ASSENGERS CAN ALSO TACTFULLY EXPRESS THEIR discomfort *when the driver is not behaving courteously*. It's generally not a good idea to "back seat drive" whether in the back seat or front seat. Let the driver make decisions unless he or she requests your input. Especially avoid urging last minute actions or changes which could confuse or fluster a driver, possibly causing a sudden change of action or direction which could cause a crash, unless you become aware of an imminent danger.

If you have a spouse or a parent or child who encourages you to drive more aggressively, tell them that is not the proper behavior for a passenger, no matter what the relationship. Aggressive drivers are the problem. Safe and courteous drivers are not the problem, they are just being considerate of the safety of the passengers, themselves and other drivers and pedestrians. If the person persists, arrange not to drive with that person in the future, unless you are able to completely disregard and even ignore (tune out) their remarks.

COURTESY

CONCENTRATE ON DEVELOPING PRIDE IN YOUR driving habits by being courteous and doing good deeds and driving responsibly. We should be judged by the way we drive. If we drive aggressively, thinking that we are entitled without being considerate, it could mean that we have a poor image of ourselves in one aspect, and our true character is coming out. On the other hand, it could mean that we have an unrealistically inflated image of ourselves, thus feeling entitled. Driving in a responsible, peaceful and forgiving spirit is a better, healthier and safer way to drive.

- Never block a driveway, intersection, alleyway or exit or entrance to a parking lot. Be careful if you stop to allow a car to enter, cross, or turn, or a pedestrian to cross. Be aware that a car coming in the other lane in your direction, or from the opposite direction, may fail to stop and you might actually have unintentionally created a potentially dangerous situation. While courtesy is important, you have to use judgment in regards to not putting in jeopardy the car or driver or the pedestrian to which you are extending courtesy.

- A four way stop sign, or even a three way stop sign, means that everyone stops in response to the sign. It is customary to let the car on the right proceed first if several cars come to the stop at the same time. Otherwise the first one to stop goes first, but remember, in actuality, no one truly has the right-of-way. *Everybody has an obligation to avoid an accident. It is illegal for more than one car to proceed after stopping at a stop sign. Each car must stop at the stop sign before proceeding.*

- If you are leaving a parking lot or entering an expressway, and there are several lanes converging, it is customary courtesy for each car in the main lane to let in one car from the converging lane.

- Always give pedestrians the right of way whether or not they are in a crosswalk. In most states it is illegal for a car to enter a crosswalk if a pedestrian is in the crosswalk. Some states permit going through the crosswalk if the pedestrian has already passed the car's path, heading for the other side. Many courteous drivers will even stop if a pedestrian is about to enter the crosswalk but has not yet stepped into it. That is actually the law in some states. You can often judge whether a pedestrian is not paying attention and therefore might walk out in front of your car, or whether they are aware of your approaching, and have slowed or stopped to wait for you to pass as they are approaching the crosswalk. In every instance, be prepared to stop if necessary. Eye contact between driver and pedestrian is helpful, as are friendly hand gestures.

- When the weather is bad and it is raining or snowing, or dangerously windy, even if pedestrians are crossing in the middle of the street, give them the courtesy of stopping, since you would want the same courtesy if you were a pedestrian under adverse weather conditions. **Pedestrians do need to extend courtesy to cars as well**.

> **When there is basically room for a car going straight and also for a car behind you to turn right on red, if you are the car that is going straight, try to stay reasonably close to the center lane, or to the center line, so that you allow space for cars to turn right after stopping for a red light or stop sign, particularly if they have indicated by signaling that they want to turn right. Sometimes moving forwards a foot or two will create space for a car or cars behind you to be able to turn right on red after stopping for a stop sign or red light.**

This car is not centered enough to allow the
car behind to turn right on red.

- If a car on your right or left is signaling that they need to change lanes to get in front of you in order to get into your lane to make a turn, or to possibly exit, be courteous and allow drivers to do that, as you would hope that they would do for you.

- Show consideration in allowing drivers who have been waiting to try to get into a lane of traffic, coming out of a driveway or parking lot. This would especially apply if you can't go far beyond that point anyway because traffic has stopped for a light in front of you. There is a tendency to not want to hold up the cars behind you by stopping, but since the traffic has stopped in front of you, the cars behind you will also have to stop and wait for the light to change. The other cars behind you will usually understand your courtesy. **Remember "courtesy is contagious"** and leads toward safer, more pleasant and less stressful driving.

- If you have an SUV, truck, or a van and there is a car waiting to turn right on red, or waiting to turn right or left at a stop sign, don't pull up so far alongside that you block their view from either side. Stay a foot or two behind so that the driver can see oncoming traffic from your side. If you are approaching a stop sign, stopping alongside and even somewhat behind an SUV or van or small truck may also allow you a better view of traffic coming from their side, especially if they have un-tinted windows.

- Go through puddles at a slow speed, lessening the likelihood of splashing pedestrians or drivers unloading trucks or getting out of cars.

Treat malfunctioning lights as a 4-way stop. Remember that some drivers may not realize that the traffic lights are not functioning, or even that there are traffic lights at that intersection. In other words, don't assume that everyone is going to stop. In some instances there may be stop signs temporarily posted at each entrance to the intersection. In all these situations, be very careful, come to a full stop, then gradually proceed when it is safe to do so.

- When a light has changed to a left turn arrow, as an example, or actually for any other light change, if you are a lead (front) vehicle, hesitate just long enough to be sure that entering the intersection is safe. That may be one or two seconds to be certain that cross traffic is stopping and there are not any emergency vehicles. If you are *not* the lead car, try not to have too great a distance between you and the car in front of you. Keep a safe distance, but not so far behind that you deprive other cars from being able to go through the turn on the arrow, or the intersection, with the light. **Always watch for approaching emergency vehicles.**
- When cars have pulled over and stopped for an emergency vehicle, let the cars in front of you that have stopped, go ahead of you, when starting up.
- If you do find yourself partially blocking a driveway or parking lot exit or entrance, be aware that if you pull up just a little bit, or back up safely, you can allow the car behind you to turn right into the driveway or you can allow a car to exit the parking lot.
- When in parking lots of large events such as sporting events, you might be directed to pull alongside another car, and if the other car's passengers haven't yet exited, but they were ahead of you and

seem to be getting ready to exit, wait a minute until they do exit, so that you don't bang doors.

- If you tend to drive such that you make eye contact with other drivers, (not referring to road rage) or pedestrians or tend to signal appropriately, there is a advantage of not having tinted windshields and front side windows. Actually tinting the windshield and the front windows is illegal in many jurisdictions unless there are medically documented serious eye problems or other health problems. I think it is important to consider the safety factor for police officers who may be making a traffic stop, i.e. being able to clearly see the driver and passengers.

- The other disadvantage of having tinted windshields and windows is that if you need help, you can't easily indicate that unless you exit your vehicle. Also you may not be able to see an intruder who has entered your parked car and is hiding in the back seat.

- When you are turning right on red, and a pedestrian has crossed in front of you while you are waiting to turn, be sure that they are not then crossing the street into which you are turning.

- When you are trying to merge, use your signals if you are merging into a lane of traffic, and if necessary wait for a car to slow down or otherwise indicate for you to go ahead. **Remember to turn off your turn signals after a lane change or expressway entrance or exit, or a half turn (into or from a diagonal street).**

- Always be courteous to pedestrians, and remember that you are a pedestrian as soon as you leave your car.

- When you see that a lane is closed, don't drive up along side and to the front of all the cars that have been waiting in the open lane, and then try to squeeze in. Rather try to merge into the adjacent open lane at a reasonable time and place where your sense of fairness will be evident to other drivers.

- It is important to be especially careful and courteous in construction zones, where construction workers and cars and trucks might be present, as well as barriers and altered roadways.

- Be particularly careful of stalled cars and police and other emergency vehicles that have stopped to assist or otherwise connect with a stalled vehicle on the side of the road. In Illinois and in most, if not all, other states there is a law that states **you must move over a lane, or if that is impossible to do, at least substantially slow down as you carefully pass the special situation.** This repetition is for important emphasis.

- Be aware of pedestrians who might be walking or running on the "wrong" side of the road (i.e. actually on your right side, in the same direction in which you are headed), or pedestrians in hospital zones and other areas such as nursing homes where pedestrians might be elderly, infirm or disabled and moving slowly. This is especially true at night and when pedestrians are wearing dark clothing.

When we are driving we tend to think that we are anonymous. We should drive as if there is a sign, my name is so and so, and I live at the following address; then I think everybody would be a much better driver. (We should also drive as if there is a parent, or other most cherished person, and/or a friendly police officer in the car watching out for our safety.)

While it is illegal to drive without insurance, you might imagine how you would drive if you didn't have any, in which case you would likely be more patient, cautious, and courteous.

MAINTENANCE

Probably most important in maintenance is to read the owners manual for your car and to be familiar with the requirements for maintenance as well as the operation of the car. Checking oil, as well as coolant and wiper fluid are things that are not difficult, and everyone could learn to do that. Many have routine maintenance at a dealer or a trusted mechanic and these items will be checked at that time also. Tires are very important to check and there might be someone in the family who does that for the other members. It may help to have a funnel when adding windshield wiper fluid.

I F YOU NOTICE OIL SPOTS UNDER your parked car, whether outside or in the garage, call that to the attention of whoever services your car. An engine could be low on oil without obvious leaking. Observe and understand urgent maintenance symbols that light up on the dash (the instrument panel) and if you don't know the significance (from the owners manual) call the service department of your dealership, or your mechanic.

Most of us will add windshield wiper fluid between regular maintenance by a mechanic or a dealer, and it is really not difficult to check the oil (consult the owner's manual). See the chapter on tires regarding checking tire pressure. Brakes should be in good working order. The exhaust system should also be in good working order for the safety of the driver and the occupants as well as other cars and the environment in general. Many states have emission control regulations requiring the vehicle to be tested periodically to be sure that its emissions are within acceptable limits.

> **The condition of the fan belts, hoses and other important items should be checked periodically by whoever is responsible for maintenance of the car. Besides tires and lights, the shocks and suspension are among other safety factors that should periodically be checked.**

If you don't have another member of the family or a friend who can put on the brake to see if the brake lights work, if you are in a parking lot with plate glass windows, usually if you are facing away, you can check them by looking in the mirror to see the reflection of the lights in the plate glass window.

TIRES

TIRES ARE THE CARS CONTACT WITH the pavement and therefore are an extremely important safety feature of a car. Some authorities say that an average tire lasts about 44,000 miles. Tire life probably depends more upon how you drive, and how closely you follow the tire inflation guide posted on the car door edge, or the door post, or glove box door, or inside of the trunk lid, or the lid for the fuel filler cover, or the car owner's manual. It also depends to some extent on whether you rotate your tires regularly. I've had cars that needed new tires after 20,000 miles, and these were not muscle cars, but the original tires were considered "performance tires." It is best not to go by the number of miles, but rather to rely on checking the tread remaining on the tires.

> The most common way to check the tire tread is to put a penny in the tread. If you can see the top of Lincoln's head, then you need to replace the tire. This means that the tread is down to or less than 1/16th of an inch. Some authorities have suggested that tires should be replaced when you can see the head of George Washington on a quarter, and this is closer to 2/16th of an inch. NHTSA recommends 1/16th of an inch. Some tires have "tread wear indicators" which show when the tire should be replaced. Generally, tread wear indicators are set to 1/16th of an inch. They look like narrow strips of smooth rubber across the tread which will appear on the tire when the tread is worn down to 1/16th of an inch. At that point, the tire is "worn out," and should be replaced.

Always check your car owner's manual for information on new or replacement tires.

It is not only the tread, but also the sidewalls which can be key areas of tire safety. If there are deep nicks, bulges or cuts, or even cracks on the sidewall, then one should consider at least having the tire checked by a competent mechanic or tire expert to see if it should be replaced.

> Under-inflation or over-inflation creates excessive stress and can lead to tire failure. This could result in vehicle damage and/or serious injury or death. An over-inflated tire can cause uneven wear in the center of the tread and also could make the tire more susceptible to road hazards and create issues with vehicle handling. Proper inflation of the tires is important and while some recommend that pressure be checked more often, I think once a month is probably more realistic, unless you regularly drive great distances, or drive the car all day, every or most days. Air is lost through a tire at the rate of approximately one pound of pressure per month, although it may be as much as 1.5 lbs. psi (pounds per square inch) per month because air escapes the tires and rims naturally. Altitude changes and changes in the air temperature can also affect the tires inflation pressure. Because of this, under-inflation would more likely be expected in the fall and winter, and over-inflation in the spring and summer. Regular checking with a good gauge is the best and safest approach at any time.

Tires can lose air suddenly if you drive over a pot hole or other object, or if you strike a high curb hard while parking or driving, or if you hit a sharp object (especially a board with protruding nails). A loose nail will often stay in the tire and the leak may be slow.

Although nitrogen stabilizes the tire pressure longer than air, it is often an extra cost, and not always conveniently available.

> Ideally every time you get into your car, you should take a walk-around and note any tire that may look low. Again it has been pointed out that a tire can be inflated to only 50% of what it should be, and still appear either normal or just slightly low. So, while not nearly as accurate as a good tire gauge, at least you will pick up an obviously low or really flat tire, by a walk-around.

If your car has a tire pressure monitoring system, this should warn you on the instrument panel with a low air pressure indicator light. Ordinarily this would be activated if one or more tires are 25% below the recommended pressure. For many vehicles, the warning on the dash may be too late to prevent damage caused by under-inflation. Tire pressure monitoring systems are helpful and actually have saved lives, but they are still not considered a replacement, rather an adjunctive measure, to monthly or regular tire pressure checks with a gauge. TPMs should probably be replaced after 10 years. If it is sooner than that, and one seems to be defective, it seems reasonable to replace just that one. Although the inexpensive stick gauges that most of us have used in the past for checking tire pressure are useful, I think it is an excellent idea to obtain a professional grade gauge, either digital or dial, which will likely be more accurate. Stick gauges can vary depending upon the position of the valve and even the gauge when you check the tire, as well as other factors.

The tire pressure should be checked when the tires are cold, i.e. not having been driven for at least three hours, and not having been driven more than a mile to a compressed air source. If you have to check tires that are "hot", i.e. after the car has been driven for a while, the pressure will read approximately 4 lbs. per square inch (p.s.i.) higher than if they were "cold". If you are checking a tire after it has been driven over a mile, and therefore is "hot", and it reads the correct recommended amount, you actually need to add 4 more lbs. p.s.i., or wait until the tire is "cold" to check the pressure. Don't forget to occasionally check your spare tire to be certain that there is adequate air in it. Be careful not to overinflate a "compact" spare tire. Check your car owner's manual for the recommended pressure.

It is a good idea to periodically check your tires for nails, embedded glass or rocks, or any other item which might ultimately damage your tire. Check the sidewalls for cracks, bulges and exposed material. When sidewalls are damaged in a blow out or an accident, or by puncture, or if the edge of the tread is damaged, often the tire will need to be replaced, rather than repaired.

NHTSA (National Highway Transportation Safety Administration) website (safercar.gov) has a number of sections on automotive safety, including an excellent one on tires.

Do not follow the pressure listed on the sidewall of the tire. For correct tire pressure, you need to follow your owner's manual or the placard or sticker in the locations mentioned.

Check your owner's manual for information on how frequently the tires on your vehicle should be rotated, as well as the preferred pattern for rotation. Tires should be balanced to avoid vibration or shaking. A wheel alignment adjusts the angles of the wheels so that they are positioned correctly relative to the vehicles frame. This adjustment maximizes the life of your tires and prevents your car from veering to the right or left when driving on a straight and level road. These adjustments require special equipment and should be performed by a qualified mechanic. Often, after tires are replaced, or an unusual object is struck with great force, alignment as well as balancing might be recommended.

Tires must always be removed from the rim to be properly inspected before being "plugged and patched" (repaired). The letters on the side of the tire indicate a number of features of the tire. Often the first letter of a passenger car or cross-over utility tire starts with P, and the next two or three digits will indicate the width of the tire in millimeters.

Uneven tread wear indicates the need to take your car in for a service inspection to check for wheel misalignment or a need for tire rotation or both. Watch for recalls on defective tires and if you think you have a defective tire, also check to see if there is a safety investigation on that particular tire. You can also find out what other consumer complaint reports are in NHTSA's database. **Although many of us tend to put aside recall notices, they can be extraordinarily important when it comes to your car, as well as some other items in our lives.**

Tire aging is another important consideration. The structural integrity of a tire can lessen over an extended period of time and that can lead to a catastrophic failure which could even lead to a crash. The aging process can be accelerated by heat and sunlight and occurs faster in warmer climates. Poor storage conditions and infrequent use can hasten the aging process.

Tire aging is generally not an issue with vehicles that are driven regularly, since tires will wear out and ordinarily will be replaced before aging becomes a safety concern. Tires with occasional use such as on recreational vehicles or collector's cars for example could be more susceptible. The spares on all vehicles are also prone to aging problems because they are seldom used or replaced. Even though the tire still has a great deal of remaining tread, the structural integrity may be at risk and the tire may be potentially hazardous even though an expert inspection may not always show the extent of tire deterioration. Vehicle owners are encouraged to have their tires checked after five years of use, and annually thereafter.

> You can determine the age of a tire by checking the tire identification number on the sidewall of the tire which begins with the letters "DOT." The last four digits of the number represent the week and year the tire was manufactured. If the tire was made before 2000 there will be three digits and the first two digits represent the week and the last digit is the year, such as 96 or 94. 464 would be the forty-sixth week of 1994. If a tire was made after 1999, the last two digits are the year and the first two are the week. On newer tires, the tire identification number is on the outside sidewall which is much more convenient. It is best not to purchase a tire that is over two years old. Some recommend that tires be replaced every six years regardless of use. Some tire manufacturers indicate 10 years as a maximum service life for tires and you can check your owner's manual for specific recommendations for your vehicle. Remember it is always better to err on the side of caution and safety, especially if you suspect your vehicle has tires that are over six years of age.

Although tire failures may result in rather minor property damage, NHTSA estimates that about 400 fatalities annually may have been attributed to tire failures.

Studded tires are allowed in some states on certain types of equipment, and in some states there are only certain times of the year when they are permissible. Other states prohibit them altogether since they do tend to cause considerable wear on the roadways. Check with your own state's Rules of the Road, produced by the Secretary of State or Department of Transportation (DOT).

Tread Separation

> If you hear a repetitive flapping sound, although it could indicate a blow out, it could also mean that you've had tread separation and you may be on the way to losing your tread. If the flapping sound stops, the tread may have already separated. Stop as soon as safely possible if you hear this sound, and inspect your tires.

So called "run flat tires" will enable you, in case of a flat tire, to drive up to 50 miles at up to 50 mph to find a place to have your spare tire put on, or the tire repaired. While this may offer some advantages, the comments of some experts on these tires are that they "run harder" and are less comfortable. However, they do seem to be improving in these aspects.

It is felt to be a misconception that lowering the air pressure inside your tires will increase your traction on ice or snow (unless they happen to be over inflated to begin with).

> Remember your tires are one of the most important safety aspects of your car and it is important to pay close attention to "where the rubber meets the road."

Flat Tire

Some drivers will carry a self-sealing, self-inflating pressurized canister instead of a spare tire. If you are in a particularly bad situation, this might enable you to go on for a short distance to a service station or other safer place to have the tire repaired or replaced. Choose non-flammable canisters. You still might need to add air with an inflator that plugs into the cigarette lighter or similar electrical source in order to increase the pressure enough to safely drive to a repair facility. The trend with newer cars is to eliminate the spare tire, and provide a kit with a sealer and an inflator. While both of these items may be helpful in certain situations, I prefer to also have a spare, even if it is a temporary spare. AAA agrees a spare tire is preferable. A sealant and an inflator are unlikely to work on a blowout or sidewall puncture or damage.

If you have used a pressurized canister with a sealant, ask whoever repairs the tire to clean the tire pressure monitor if your car is so equipped. Current pressurized sealants should not gum-up your tire pressure monitor. Check the label on your pressurized sealant. If necessary, get new current pressurized sealant.

It is very helpful to have an automobile club card, something that some of the major car manufacturers also offer, providing roadside service. AAA is one of the older more established and reliable services and I have been satisfied with their road service over nearly three decades. There are now many different services where you can have somebody come and change your tire. You can change it yourself if you are so inclined, and in a safe spot. It is a good idea for new drivers to learn how to change a tire, but it is very important that they are certain that they are in a very safe spot to do this. Changing a tire on the driver's side, jutting out into the roadway, creates a very dangerous situation. If you do plan to change the tire yourself, you should read your driver's manual carefully and probably should practice it in your driveway or other safe location, so that you feel somewhat comfortable in case you do have to do it on the road. Always carry reflective triangles in case of a breakdown from any cause, and know how to set them up. Practice that ahead of the usage. I recommend keeping two or three triangles already set up, lying flat in your trunk, to expedite their use. You will still need to turn the base to make a stable cross, an act that should only take 5-10 seconds for each triangle.

You will need a jack, jack handle, and suitable wrench which could be the jack handle, to loosen the lugs on the tire. Often when tires are installed professionally, the lugs are so tightened that it is often difficult for a person without special equipment to loosen them. You should ask that they be tightened but not beyond that which an average person, or perhaps particularly you, would be able to remove the lugs. Remember to keep your car's manual in the car at all times. Always check the manual to see where the jack can be safely placed on the car. You need to loosen the lug nuts while the tire still firmly contacts the ground even though you may have raised it somewhat. You then raise the tire completely off the ground, remove the lugs and wheel with tire, and replace it with the spare, put the lugs back on and tighten them until snug but not all the way, then lower the jack until the tire is in firm contact with the ground, tighten the lugs all the way and remove the jack. Change on level ground, put the parking brake on, and be sure the engine is off, and the gear is in park. Some recommend blocking a wheel.

The best tool for me has always been a four-way crossbar, with different sizes of lug nut openings, and most people of average strength are able to get pretty good torque (leverage) using that.

In terms of eliminating the spare tire, I think it might be more important to remove unnecessary items from the trunk and elsewhere in the car. If the readers of this book have had experience with the above, particularly if they have any other thoughts, I would appreciate if they would contact me at P.O. Box 308, Wilmette, IL 60091. The purpose of this would be to include experience and suggestions in any future editions, and any potential contributors should include written permission to include their name and town, if they wish.

GAS REFUELING

A LTHOUGH THIS CHAPTER DEALS WITH REFUELING with gasoline presently, in the future there will be more use of alternative fuels such as natural gas, hydrogen fuel cells, and electricity, this latter often being used in conjunction with another form of fuel for the motor, as in a hybrid.

If you are driving on the highway, especially if you are unfamiliar with the area, don't wait until your gas tank is too far down before looking for a gas station. If the weather is particularly cold, or snowy, or there are unusual traffic conditions (major traffic jams), or in emergency situations such as hurricanes and other natural or man made disasters, you might want to keep the gas tank as full as possible all the time. As mentioned earlier, in cold weather, a car with a full gas tank is less likely to freeze up, and secondly, in case you are stranded for hours on an expressway or freeway, you are in better shape starting with a full tank. **Running out of gas is the most common disability of a car, and ordinarily should be avoidable.**

> When you are filling up your gas tank, you should turn off the motor, put the car in park, apply the emergency (parking) brake, and take the keys out of the car, and lock the car even if you do not leave the pump to go inside the station to pay for gas, purchase Lotto tickets, or other items, or use the restroom. This habit lessens the possibility that your car will be stolen while you are in the station, or that an unwelcome attacker or carjacker will be waiting inside your car when you return, or that an item such as a purse will be stolen.

Drive slowly and carefully while in gas stations, especially backing up, and be aware of other drivers walking to pay for gas or to purchase Lotto tickets or other items, or to use the restrooms. **Stay alert while refueling.**

If you have a rental car or another car that you are unfamiliar with, such as a loaner car from a dealership while your car is being serviced, check to see on which side (or rear of the car) that the gas tank refueling opening is on, before you drive, just to expedite your refueling. In some cars this will be indicated on the dash. The gas tank opening may even be behind a hinged rear license plate. Ask the person loaning or renting the car to show you, if necessary. On some newer cars the gas tank cap is replaced with a cover that is attached to the lid for the opening. There is a flap-like opening and you should be sure that you are comfortable with this before you drive the car out of the rental station or the dealership. You can check with the gas station attendant if one is available. I've had one experience where I could not read the instructions on the pump until I took off my sunglasses. This happened where the window through which instructions are viewed was scratched, and is probably an unlikely scenario, but happened with polarized sunglass lenses.

I've also had the experience that once I set up to put gas in the car, I couldn't open the cover for the gas tank because it was frozen. A year or so later, I couldn't open it even with warm weather, because of misalignment. The dealership fixed it.

I strongly recommend that when you refuel, you not have small children strapped into the car in booster or infant seats. If there happens to be a fire or a car jacking, it would be much more difficult to safely remove them. It is safest to refuel when you are the only person present, or the passengers are mobile and alert adults or older children. It is also recommended that you stay outside the car, attending to the filling, and most stations post this request.

If while refueling, you do go back inside the car because of cold or adverse weather, when you again get out of your car, you should touch something metal to discharge the static electricity caused by scooting across the car seat. This is actually also good to do when you first get out, i.e. you should touch something metal before you begin to refuel. Often there are convenient round protective metal bars near the pumps, or you can discharge the static electricity by touching the outside of the driver's side door. The further away you are from the gas tank, particularly an open gas tank, the better.

Many authorities caution not only against using cell phones, but even having them on your person, while you are re-fueling. Some advise that ideally cell phones should be left in the car. Many service stations post instructions such as no smoking, and to turn off cellular phones. Some authorities have stated that just having your phone ring while you are re-fueling can create a spark significant enough to ignite gas fumes. While some considered this an urban myth, there may have been suggestive instances of the above. This remains controversial.

Perhaps also somewhat in the category of an urban myth is advice that "Besides cell phones, it is advised that all portable battery operated devices should be shut off before refueling." This is often posted on major service station instructions on the fuel pumps or nearby.

If a fire does occur, the usual advice is to not take the pump out of the gas tank, but instead notify the filling station attendant.

In 2016 I did a survey of a number of service stations in the Chicago suburbs. In some, the kill switch was inside, and in some it was outside and in one it was in both locations. There is a small red button to stop the gas flow on the front of some newer gasoline pumps. It is a good idea to be aware of the location of the shut off switch, and/or the training of the attendants in the unlikely event of a pump fire or pump malfunction.

I also contacted one station where the person answering the phone stated that it was their first day and they didn't know the answer. Another responded that I or they would have to talk to the owner who wasn't there. Forewarned is forearmed. This is another reason that it is best to not have anybody in the car when you are refueling, especially small children or elderly parents or friends.

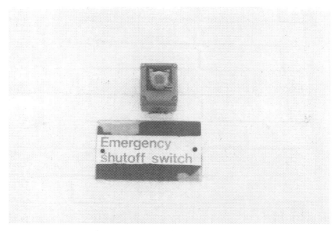

An emergency refueling cut-off switch outside of a station.

It is important to extinguish all cigarettes (smoking while driving, *and in general* is strongly discouraged). Don't take the pump out of the gas tank until you see on the pump dial that the flow of gas has stopped. The click that you may hear from another pump might be mistaken for your pump. Look at your pump as it is recording the gas amount and the total charged to be sure the flow has in fact stopped. If your hand is on the pump handle, you should be able to feel and hear the pump clicking off. **Topping off is definitely discouraged**.

Although a busy and well lit gas station is a relatively safe place, there have been attempted robberies and car-jacking, and other illegal acts, and even fires, so it is a good idea to be alert.

Be certain that you replace the gas cap and close the door to the gas tank compartment.

At the end of the refueling procedure, there is often a question as to whether or not you want a receipt, and you want to be sure that the question you are answering is not whether or not you want a car wash if offered, since if you don't want a car wash, there will be an extra charge if you push "yes."

At the end of 2012 and beginning of 2013 AAA pointed out that although the EPA had approved E15 (15% Ethanol and 85% gasoline) for flex fuel and many other cars, a number of manufacturers have stated that the corrosive effect of this fuel mix will void warranties on some of their cars. Owners are urged to read precautions listed on the gasoline pumps and sometimes on the gas cap. Your owner's manual should also have directions on the proper fuels that can be used in your vehicle.

SHARING THE ROAD
WITH MOTORCYCLES

T HE MOST IMPORTANT ASPECT OF SHARING the road with motorcycles for the car driver is to be aware of their presence. Motorcycles can come up very fast, and they may, depending upon how you have your mirrors set and the length of the motorcycle, be invisible in your left side view mirror blind spot, as well as your right side view mirror blind spot. That is one of the reasons I recommend keeping a constant watch on both sides, the rear view and the front, so that you, at all times as the car driver, know what is around you, or coming up in any lane.

> Remember that a motorcycle can stop much quicker than you, so don't follow a motorcycle closely. Motorcycles are given the same respect that a car would have in a lane, and you should only pass a motorcycle in another lane. This is in contrast to a bicycle that might be on the side of the road and where you might pass it in your lane, with at least a three- foot clearance.

If your windows are open and your hearing is good, often you will be aware of motorcycles because they will frequently create more noise than cars. By law, they are supposed to have their front light on, and often when you see a single light, that's a motorcycle, unless it is a car with one headlight burned out. That's a problem because you may assume at night that that's a motorcycle and you may not allow the distance necessary to avoid a crash. This is another reason for checking your headlights and replacing the ones that are burned out. Some motorcycles have twin headlights, and usually there will be turn signal lights on either side of the single or double headlights, as well as on the back. In the future, in fact they are working on that as I'm writing this, there may be electric motorcycles, and the awareness of those will be more difficult because of the absence of the characteristic noise, unless it is artificially created.

In most accidents involving a motor vehicle and a motorcycle, the motorcycle rider is severely injured, often fatally. It is extremely important to not change lanes and force an unseen motorcycle to "wipe out." Also, as you and your passengers are exiting your car, be certain that there are no bicyclists or motorcyclists that the car door opening might force into an accident.

Motorcycles ideally would not ride two abreast in the same lane, but unfortunately you'll encounter that situation, and it is legal in many states. Each motorcycle should command and occupy an entire lane, or at least ride in a staggered position, or single file formation for greater safety.

Most motorcyclists are law obeying, careful drivers, wearing helmets, gloves, leather or denim jackets and pants, and boots or heavy shoes. Some will have no helmets or gloves, wearing tee shirts and shorts, and sneakers, but will still be law abiding.

We have all encountered motorcyclists who were "hot dogging" in the sense that they were speeding and narrowly cutting in front of cars, weaving in and out, and driving between two cars in adjacent lanes, needlessly revving their engines. Fortunately, these are in the minority, but California has somewhat condoned "lane splitting" if the cars are slowly moving or stopped, and may even make it legal.

An older motorcycle's turn signals may not always automatically turn off, so don't depend on a motorcycle (or a car) turning just because their turn signals indicate that. As mentioned before, car drivers may forget to turn off a turn signal after a lane change or a half turn into an angle (diagonal) street, or after pulling out from a parallel parking space.

SHARING THE ROAD
WITH BICYCLISTS

Bicyclists are supposed to obey the rules of the road, but in my experience, that's unfortunately the exception. I see bicyclists almost predictably going through stop signs and red lights, driving between cars, going the wrong way on a one- way street, and doing all of this without lights, or helmets, or reflectors or other important safety considerations. There are some bicyclists who are well versed in the right way, and they are usually recognizable by their dress, equipment, and actions.

B ICYCLISTS ARE NOT SUPPOSED TO DRIVE two abreast, but I've encountered this frequently. Although a bicyclist might choose to occupy a lane, generally they will be on the right edge of the road, and they should be in single file. When passing them, you can stay in your lane, but you should give them a minimum of at least three feet clearance, and sometimes, if the situation permits, you might even choose to cross the centerline of the roadway, if you can safely do this, in order to allow the bicyclist sufficient clearance as you pass. Otherwise hang back and wait for an opportunity to safely pass. If you are opposing a bicyclist and a driver passing the bicyclist, try to stay as far to the right as you can safely, in case the car passing the bicyclist crosses the center line to allow sufficient clearance of the bicyclist.

Be aware that small children on bicycles are subject to particular danger, and even those children who are riding on the sidewalk might suddenly go into the street. I daily see adults riding bicycles on the sidewalk, and I think that may be permitted in many areas. If they are, they need to yield the right of way to pedestrians and also if they pass a pedestrian, they need to warn them audibly. They also should be careful not to hit pedestrians exiting shops directly onto the sidewalk. Children often ride on the sidewalk, and I agree that is much safer for children. Both adults and children have come from the sidewalk to quickly enter a crosswalk at an intersection, frequently in front of a car which has stopped waiting to enter the intersection, or a car turning into the street. Sometimes this causes the turning car to stop and be in the path of oncoming traffic. Both adults and children should ideally walk bicycles across busy intersection crosswalks, and not ride, and then only when it is safe and legal, the reason being that they can usually more easily avoid an errant vehicle if walking their bicycle. When bicycles are being legally ridden in the street and they have green lights or the right of way (the cross traffic has stop signs or a red traffic signal), they need not stop or walk the bike, but proceed with caution. Bicyclists should wear reflective clothing, or a bright yellow jacket. They need reliable front and rear lights, and I think the lights that rapidly blink probably most likely gain the attention of the motorist. Be especially aware of bicycles in the summer when children are on summer vacation. The State of Illinois has enacted severe penalties for drivers that do not share the road safely with bicyclists, especially by not giving them enough room when passing. While I applaud these efforts, I think there should be similar efforts penalizing bicyclists who disobey the rules of the road.

Some bicyclists in some areas of Chicagoland have told me that in their suburb, a bicyclist can go through a stop sign or red traffic light if there is no traffic. If there are cars, they say they need to obey the traffic rules. While I can't comment on this, and this may be the custom in some jurisdictions, it seems to be illegal, at least in Illinois, and generally less safe.

BUSES

School Buses

SCHOOL BUSES ARE USUALLY YELLOW, AND have a stop sign that extends out from the front of the bus on the driver's side to indicate that traffic in both directions must stop. They will also have flashing lights that will indicate the same. You should stop well behind the school bus, and not pass it until the flashing lights have gone off and the stop sign arm has been retracted. Sometimes they will have a long, usually yellow, bar that will extend out from the front bumper, on the driver's side. It's important to hesitate long enough before starting up to be certain that there are no children crossing in front of or behind the school bus, i.e. wait for the bus to leave that stop.

If a school bus seems to be taking an unusual amount of time to load or unload, it may be that they are helping a child with a disability. Be patient in this situation.

If you are on a two lane road, you must stop behind the bus, and opposing traffic will stop in front of the bus. On a four lane roadway where a bus is stopped in the opposite direction from which you are traveling, you are not required to stop your vehicle, but you should drive with caution. I've seen instances where children would dash across all four lanes, so my advice is to know the rules of your state, and still be very cautious in that situation.

Remember to give our school children every break possible, and disobedience of the law in regards to school buses is severely punishable.

School buses must always stop at railroad crossings. They may need more room to turn, and in some intersections, may make wide right turns.

Mass Transportation Buses

Sometimes CTA or public transportation buses will go from picking up passengers in the right or curb lane, crossing all the way (two or three lanes over) to a left turn lane, so be aware. Also, some bus stops are put on the far corner rather than the near corner. It is always illegal to pass a bus to turn right in front of the bus. In Chicagoland, some suburb's mass transportation busses are permitted under certain circumstances (especially when traffic on a certain highway is moving less than 35 mph), to ride on the right shoulder.

Commercial Buses

Follow the same advice offered in the section on Trucks. Be aware of the courtesy needed to extend to buses that are loading or unloading passengers.

RENTALS AND LOANERS

WITH A RENTAL VEHICLE, OR WITH any other vehicle which you are unfamiliar with or haven't driven for a while, especially Zipcars and the other hourly rental systems that are available, it is important to familiarize yourself with the essential controls before you even start driving. When you are renting a vehicle, try to get the same vehicle that you have been driving at home, so that you know where the controls are. Some people will pick a very different automobile, just for the experience, but then they may very well struggle trying to find the controls. Most important are:

- lights
- horn
- windshield wipers
- mirrors (should be properly adjusted)
- emergency flashers
- heater
- air conditioner
- windows
- parking brake (sometimes less correctly called emergency brake), and particularly its release
- engine turn off
- car starter (key or push button)
- fog lamps (if present)
- switch for high beam lights
- defroster
- rear window defroster and defogger

Still important, but perhaps less distracting or urgent, are knowing how to operate the following:

- radio
- door locks
- gas tank cover
- gears
- hood release
- trunk release
- seat adjustment
- head rest adjustment

I think it is a good idea to check the turning radius of the car that you are renting or driving so that you will have a better feel how to safely drive it, both pulling out of a parking space, making u-turns if necessary, or even just pulling out of a driveway, or going around a corner.

Getting into any car, especially when it has been most recently driven by others, it is important to adjust all the mirrors so that you can see well, and that's covered in another chapter. The seats and the head rests should be adjusted. The horn should be checked to be sure that it works and that you know how to use it.

Be aware of the settings for headlights. With high beam headlights, there is usually a blue indicator on the instrument panel. It is most important that you know how to turn the headlights on, and be sure that you are turning on headlights and not just the parking lights. In many cars there is a little yellow icon that appears in the dash that will alert you to the fact that the headlights are for sure on. Don't forget to use headlights if you are driving in bad weather, in the evening, or in parking lots. Keeping the headlights on whenever driving, has been advised to decrease the chance of a crash. As mentioned elsewhere, daylight running lights may serve the same purpose to some extent, however, in bad weather, in the evening, or in parking lots, it is important to have your full headlights on, and in many states it is the law to have your headlights on if your windshield wipers, even interval wipers, are on.

Be aware of the height, length and width of your vehicle. If you are renting a car, in an unfamiliar area, especially in the mountains, if there is someone tailgating you, it is likely a resident native to the area, or someone else who is very familiar with the road. There are often passing lanes or viewing spots where you can turn off the road and allow the tailgater to pass, or if you stay to the right, the tailgater will usually pass when there is a passing lane.

Be sure to do a walk around and note any damage to a rental or loaner car, and make sure it is documented before you pull out of the rental car lot, or dealership.

When you get back into your car after a car wash or parking by a valet, or even after the car has been serviced, make sure that the mirrors are again adjusted so that you can see correctly, and that the seat is adjusted and anything else that was personally adjusted to fit you is back the way it was before.

If, after parking, or servicing your car, you find a parking slip or work ticket with a number on it, on the dash, remove it before driving. I have found this distracting because of a reflection on the windshield.

EMERGENCIES

Water Entrapment

> If you have ended up in water for whatever reason, either by losing control and sliding into a lagoon, retention pond, lake or other body of potentially deep water, or having an accident, or having a road or bridge go out from under you, and ending up under water, you may have a second or two where the electric windows may still be working, or you may have manual windows and you can put them down and escape through the window if necessary, if the water is deep. If you can't get the windows open, there is a spot at the lower left corner of the driver's window which if struck with enough force by a hammer or any similar punch-type tool kept in the console compartment, should shatter the window and allow you to escape through it. If you have a sunroof that is open, or can be opened, that could be another avenue of escape depending upon your size and the size of the sunroof, and your own agility.

I F EVERYTHING ELSE FAILS AND THE car is filling up, and you have thus far been unable to open the door because of the outside pressure of the water, at some point, as the car is filling up, the pressure from the water inside the car will likely equal the pressure from the water outside the car, and you may be able to force the door open to escape. It may be very difficult or impossible to open damaged or bent car doors, or when the car frame has been damaged. Remember to unlock the doors.

One hint is to try to turn yourself to the left so that you can use your legs to push on the door, and grabbing the steering wheel, you may have some leverage to push even harder against the door.

If you are underwater and you haven't been able to open the door or break the window, often there is an air pocket in the back seat. You should go to that area if all else fails, and try the maneuvers mentioned. In most cars with center consoles getting into the back seat is not easy. **Unlock your doors to aid rescuers, and leave your headlights on.** Don't forget to call 9-1-1 on your cell phone if your situation permits.

Do unhook your seatbelt as you are preparing to try to exit and if necessary, cut the seatbelt with the tool that you should have in the console. If the water is not that deep, and the current is not that strong, you might choose to stay in the car until help arrives. You usually will be able to tell early-on whether water is going to be way over the top of the car or less, i.e. the car will be stable and the water level will be visible and stable. Give instructions to any passengers in the car. In a strong current, watch for dams.

Blow Outs

It is not unusual to see a tire which has been blown out (from a truck or car) in the middle of the road. Generally, if it is just a piece of a tire and if you hit it, unless it is very large, it is not a major problem. If you can avoid it or position it so that it is in the center of your car, especially if you have a high clearance, that would be preferable. You should also report those to * 999.

There are several types of tire problems, and probably the most common is a slow leak where you might get a message on your dash (instrument panel) that your tire pressure is low, and this could be all the tires, or most often just one or two tires. You do need to check your tires and to inflate them, and if they keep losing pressure, then you need to have them checked, and repaired or replaced. If a tire is real low, it is a good idea to check it as soon as possible, since driving on it will be unsafe and it is likely something that is going to recur quickly if you just simply inflate it.

You should always look for low tires during a walk-around before you enter your car. If you become aware of a low tire while on the road, you should pull far off to the right onto the shoulder in a safe area, put your flashers on, and very carefully get out to inspect it. That's probably the most dangerous part. If you can pull into a filling station or into a well lit parking lot, that would usually be much safer.

A blow out happens fairly suddenly and you will usually hear the sound which could be a pop like a gunshot or Firecracker. Your car may indicate low pressure on the instrument panel, and may pull to the side of a blowout, especially if it is a front tire.

If that happens, you need to hold onto the wheel firmly, put on your turn signal indicating that you are pulling off to the right, and put on your flashers, brake gently, and try to pull off the road, onto the shoulder of the expressway. If you have an AAA membership or other roadside assistance membership, you can call for assistance, or the state highway department of transportation emergency vehicle will come along on an expressway or other major road and help you put your spare tire on. You can try to use your tire sealer and inflator but that may not work as well with a blow out. **You should always check to be sure your spare tire is properly inflated.** If you keep a lot of equipment, or other material in your trunk, it's good to have them in one or two duffle bags or other easy to remove containers, to facilitate easy access to your spare, especially if your spare is under the floor mat in the trunk.

> **There is another option, if you are in a spot that is very dangerous, whether it be an unfamiliar neighborhood or the traffic on the road, you might elect to find a safe spot and this could mean that you may have to drive on this blown-out tire for a considerable distance. This will often, and probably usually, ruin the tire and may even ruin the rim, but it may save lives. This is a judgment call for you to make.**

If you choose to drive with a flat tire, you need to have your flashers on to indicate that you are going slowly because you are disabled, and you should be in the right lane and exit at the first safe opportunity. If you are not familiar with the neighborhood, sometimes it is actually safer to remain on the shoulder of the expressway.

Run flat tires have been mentioned earlier. There are also tires which do not require any air. These are not yet suitable for passenger cars, and mainly, for the present, are used in some military vehicles and farm equipment. You should ordinarily carry only necessary emergency equipment in the trunk.

Ladders and Other Items Falling Off Trucks and Even Cars

Ladders, other items, and even axles have dropped off of trucks as well as cars. There may be spillage of liquid contents of various types including flammable contents. This is one reason to be very alert and to have a reasonable interval between you and the car or truck in front of you so that you will be able to successfully avoid these items falling off or leaking from trucks and cars.

Rock Slide

A rock slide or other similar obstruction which could include part of an avalanche would ordinarily only occur in a mountainous or very hilly region or in a canyon. You must be prepared to stop suddenly in those, as well as other situations. A rock slide in the mountains can close a road temporarily. Notify authorities with your cell phone.

Avalanches

An avalanche ordinarily would occur only on roads in high country, i.e. mountainous areas where there are significant amounts of snow on the mountains. An avalanche coming down upon a car will stop the car fairly quickly and you should **shut off the engine, if it hasn't stopped, to avoid the danger of carbon monoxide poisoning**. For avalanches and many other emergencies consult your mountain state's rules of the road, and I would also refer you to the details given in "*110 Car and Driving Emergencies and How to Survive Them*" by James Joseph. This can be obtained through amazon.com. Lyons Press, P.O. Box 480, Gilford, CT 06437 is the publisher.

Snow Blizzards

Like all weather related emergencies, keeping in touch with weather reports by the radio, or even by phoning the highway patrol or sheriff's office or the local weather bureau, or even the local newspaper for the latest weather advisory before starting out, is a good idea. Many drivers will use apps and Smartphones or similar devices for weather and traffic alerts.

In a severe blizzard, such as a white-out, where the wipers and defrosters don't work sufficiently, do not proceed further, but try to find shelter. This may require you turning around and going in the opposite direction, but that may not work because the storm may also be coming from that direction.

> **If you are really stuck and you can't get into a shelter, *stay* in your car. It is much more dangerous to risk venturing out into the wind and snow, with the exception possibly to tie something, such as a colorful rag or scarf to the cars antenna, if in fact your car has an antenna. Tying a handkerchief, rag, or brightly colored scarf to the driver's side door handle or just protruding out the door or window may be used to indicate the need for help. It is a good idea to keep a blaze orange or yellow cloth in the glove compartment, something that could be attached to an antenna or put in the driver,s side door handle or just protruding out the door or window as mentioned above. To attract notice from aircraft above, line up three large rocks, or any other large items, or use two with one next to the middle of the two. It is difficult to walk to a shelter, even if you can see it a few hundred yards away. In a severe storm, even venturing a few feet from your car can cause you to become lost, and therefore it is much safer to stay in the car. If you happen to have a lengthy rope, you could at least use that to get around the car to check the exhaust for blockage, and anything else that needs checking. Tie one end to the steering wheel or column, or window post, or door handle, and the other end to your waist.**

If you are young and are in particularly good physical shape, and if you are in an area where heavy snows are frequent, you might choose to keep a pair of snow shoes in your vehicle, and even a pair of ski poles. Again staying in the car is much safer, unless there is an obviously occupied home or business *very close*. Even then you have to use judgment since it might still be safer to stay in the car.

Some experts on survival in this situation suggest keeping the engine running, because if you turn the engine off or only run it intermittently, you may not be able to restart it. On the other hand, keeping the engine running risks carbon monoxide poisoning and if you do choose to run it intermittently, it is often suggested that you should accelerate the engine to a high idle, to the point where the battery gauge or indicator shows that the battery is being charged, for 15 minutes every hour, with at least one window (downwind) cracked open a few inches. The same is true in regards to the window if the engine is run continuously.

If you are stuck, don't drink alcohol and don't eat snow unless you melt it first. As mentioned in the chapter on winter conditions, you need to have some provisions in the car, probably in the trunk, and you need to take them out and put them inside the car as soon as you are stalled in a blizzard. This could include heavier clothing, non-perishable food products and especially bottled water. Also some means of allowing for passage of urine and possibly other bodily substances, however difficult, could be important. Candles, matches, and an empty coffee can may be used to melt snow.

High Winds

Listen for high wind warnings since these can seriously affect driving, particularly with high profile vehicles such as vans or trucks, SUVs and even sedans. As steering is more difficult, it is especially important to have two hands on the wheel with a strong grip when the winds are high, since you may find that your vehicle will be buffeted up to a few feet in either direction at times. Avoid having luggage or mattresses strapped onto the roof.

A large semi-trailer truck passing at high speed also creates a wind pull.

If the winds are too strong, and especially if there are adequate and serious warnings, it is best to get off the road until they subside.

Earthquakes

There usually is no warning when an earthquake occurs. The car may be one of the safest places to be, but this is especially so if you are on a highway, and not in the city next to tall buildings. Grasp the wheel firmly, and head for an open road and avoid any structure crossing a highway such as an overpass which could collapse, or it could even collapse under you if you are on it. Notify the police or emergency services if you need help.

If driving in town, try to get into the lane furthest from the curb, into the center of the street to avoid being hit by collapsing buildings or objects falling from buildings, and then try to get out into the open. You should be looking for an open space with no buildings, wires or overhangs, and no tall trees, and stop there if not obstructing traffic. Watch out for broken water or gas mains, and especially falling debris and downed power lines. Do not drive over downed power lines. Aftershocks are likely to occur.

Flash Floods

The definition of a flash flood can be either a sudden unexpected flood which could result from an extremely heavy rain, or could come subsequent to a period of heavy rain that persists for a long period of time, or even from upstream melting snow in the springtime. Ice jams, when in the river upstream or downstream can precede a flash flood. Downstream ice jams may produce river back-up with flooding.

> **A flash flood is capable of moving heavy cars, and even trucks, to their destruction. Flooding can cross roads and bridges, and run down canyons and flood anything in its low lying path, including roads and streets. More than half of the approximately 150 to 200 annual flash flood fatalities are drivers, many of them swept to their death in cars while attempting to cross a flooded road, or a dip, or a low bridge, or stream.**

Keeping in touch with sources of weather alerts, through the radio or apps, or calling ahead is one way to prevent being caught in a flash flood.

It is a good idea to stay off of unfamiliar roads and to not drive at night when the conditions might cause flash flooding.

> **Drive at a slower speed, and keep your headlights on during the day as well, if you have to drive at all. Watch out for road dips, ravines, culverts, and canyons in some areas. The flash flood may not be the result of a cloud burst in your area, but could even be from distant rain storms upstream.**

It is best not to try to cross any flooded road since what may appear to be a reasonable crossing could turn out to have dips, mud holes, or wash outs with water several feet deep. A car can be carried away in less than two feet of rushing water. Six inches of rapidly moving water can knock a person down.

If your car is carried downstream, generally it is safer to stay inside, rather than trying to jump from your car into a raging current. If the water level is coming up too high to safely stay in the car, you may have to try accessing the car roof through the window or the sunroof. You could try to catch a sturdy tree limb. Ordinarily you should stay on top of the car until you are rescued. If the water is still rising, you may have to try to swim to shore or find a tree or tree limb, especially if you are approaching going over a dam. Every situation can be different, and may depend on the depth and speed of the current. This is different than being entrapped in a retention basin or pond. Keep your headlights on and honk your horn, if possible. It is obviously far better to avoid this situation, by finding higher ground and parking, and waiting for the flood waters to recede.

Flash flooding can not only be dangerous to drivers, but also to hikers and campers. The swiftness of the lethal rise of water is remembered from years ago in the Big Thompson Canyon, near Estes Park in Colorado, and more recently along the Little Missouri River in Arkansas. Campers have been the tragic victims of unexpected flash flooding during the night. If the brakes seem to not work because they are wet, pump the brake pedal gently at first and then firmer. This may restore them faster than initially braking hard. Usually car brakes can be dried and will be working after pumping on and off ten to twelve times.

Remember if you are in a still body of water and it is not at a level that will cause drowning, you can in some instances remain in the car, or you can escape through the window as mentioned. Ordinarily in this situation, there will be a shoreline or another accessible safety spot not too far away.

Hail Storms

The size of the hail in a hail storm could be anywhere from pea or marble size to golf ball or even softball size or larger. If you can, pull under some type of shelter or into a parking garage. If you are not near anything of that nature to pull into, try to find a viaduct or bridge to pull under. A tree may offer some protection against damage to you car, however if there is lightning, it is advisable to not park under a tree. Most of the time the main danger from a hail storm is damage to the car.

I would again refer interested drivers to the book by James Joseph, *"110 Car and Driver Emergencies and How to Survive Them"* which goes into more detail, especially regarding weather related and other emergencies. It is best to avoid these situations, and if you are in any kind of emergency situation, remember to keep a firm grip on the steering wheel and usually to brake gently rather than suddenly, again depending upon circumstances.

Tornado

Listening to the radio or checking weather sources may help you to avoid tornados. It is better to not drive at night if the weather is threatening.

> **If you hear a warning of a tornado in your area, you should immediately seek shelter, as opposed to a tornado watch, in which case you may also want to seek shelter. That may not be as immediately necessary and you may want to just continue getting reports. It is important to read this entire section on tornadoes.**

If you are in a city, try to find shelter underground, in a public building, or any sturdy structure, preferably one that will have a basement.

If nothing else is available, a small windowless room is preferable to a large area. In a house, occupants are often recommended to go underneath a staircase leading from the first floor to the basement, or if there is no basement, again a small windowless room on the lowest floor.

If you are on the highway, and there are no buildings, try to avoid an open area. If you can, find a large drainage pipe like a culvert that runs beneath or beside roads, or a ditch off of the far edge of the shoulder. Any area below ground level will offer some protection. If you can not locate any of the above shelters, get out of your car, because a car is felt to be the least safe place to be. Lie face down in an open space, preferably a ditch, and cover your head with your hands to protect against blowing debris. **Don't try to outrun an approaching tornado**. If you are very familiar with the terrain and you see a tornado approaching and you go at right angles to it, you may or may not be able to avoid it. It is much better to seek appropriate shelter.

Many drivers will think that with eight or nine airbags and seatbelts, a car might be the safest place, but most every authority recommends leaving the car and placing yourself in the lowest possible location.

Car and Truck Fires

It is not unusual for a car or truck to catch on fire and there can be a variety of reasons that this happens. A well maintained and frequently inspected car is less likely to catch on fire.

Although the number of vehicle fires decreased considerably from 1993 to 2003, I hear radio traffic reports almost every day about a car or truck on fire in Chicagoland and the surrounding driving area. The possible decrease is felt to be due to the automakers and suppliers' efforts to increase safety and reliability of vehicle components. But nevertheless there have been a number of recalls which have involved components of cars or even engines catching on fire. A significant number of reported vehicle fires are in vehicles that aren't even involved in a crash.

There are some things that you can do to avoid the chance of a vehicle fire.

- Have your vehicle maintained regularly and emphasize to a trusted mechanic that you want to avoid any kind of break down, including a fire. Your car should be checked by a competent mechanic at least once a year.

- Get a mechanical inspection after even what looks like a simple fender bender. Be aware that a relatively minor rear-ender may have dislodged an important and vital component or structure and may create a potentially dangerous situation. While this is not likely, still you do want to play it safe and you don't want to be the one pulled off on the side of a highway with a fire.

- **Have electrical accessories installed by a specialist.** Only let highly qualified technicians install high powered audio equipment or other accessories in your car, or if they are not professional, at least make sure they have a very, very thorough understanding of automotive electrical systems.

> - **Do not smoke in the car. Smoking still causes many avoidable vehicle fires. Not smoking will cut your chances of being involved in a fire. Smoking is also a serious distraction since it occupies one arm and hand, and also cigarette ashes can fall on upholstered or leather car seats, often distracting the driver. Many states are banning smoking if there are younger passengers, because of health concerns with passive cigarette smoke exposure, not necessarily because of the fire hazard, which, as has been mentioned earlier, could seriously complicate an accident.**

- Watch out for oil leaks. In an automotive situation, while oil might not ordinarily catch on fire, it could reach its flash point. Oil leaks could lead to a fire and therefore should be fixed.

- Headlights that dim when you turn on your rear defogger or other accessories might indicate an electrical problem in the car, something which needs to be checked out.

- A Halon fire extinguisher could be used inside the car, as could a regular fire extinguisher rated A, B and C (oil, gas and electrical fires, and burning items that can be extinguished with water). Halon fire extinguishers were banned by the government because of the effect on the ozone layer. However, they are still available and one could Google auto fire extinguishers or even Halon fire extinguishers. There is a more recent one which uses a propellant which is environmentally safe. They are available, especially through Auto Sports and possibly other sources and you could Google that as well. This might be especially appropriate if you or passengers are trapped in the car, or so injured that removal from a burning car is dangerous. If you are involved in an accident, you may not be able to open the doors, especially if the frame is bent. It might be difficult, but important, to *securely* attach a fire extinguisher to an accessible spot inside of the car, especially in the front of the car, so that it doesn't become a dangerous object in case of a crash. The advantage of a Halon or newer similar approved type is that it does not leave a residue which is difficult to clean up, and is less harmful to the car occupants. Some might choose to also have a fire extinguisher securely affixed in the trunk of the car, although that would be most useful in helping to put out a fire in another car.

One third of the people hurt in vehicle fires were injured while trying to control the fire. Having a fire extinguisher could lead to a false sense of security.

Don't try to stay with the car if you can get out, and don't try to put anything out but a small interior fire with the fire extinguisher (and even that may not eliminate the danger of an explosion). It's best to get far away and call for help.

If your car is on fire with visual flames, then especially you need to pull over to the side immediately, signaling so that you can safely do so, putting your flashers on at the same time. Don't worry about the car, just pull off the road. Get as far as possible to the right side so that you don't get hit by a passing car. If there is a wall or fence on the right, leave yourself room so that you and any passengers can get out on the passenger side. Most experts advise against quickly popping up the hood because that may make an engine fire much worse and may be very dangerous to the person opening the hood. You should get as far away as you can, and call 9-1-1 and report a car or truck fire at your location. A car can be replaced, you can't be.

If you just see smoke from under the hood, stop immediately and turn off the ignition, because the car itself may soon catch on fire. Again all passengers and the driver should leave the car and stay a safe distance away. If, in a few minutes, the smoke dies down, you could carefully open the hood, making sure that the latch is not hot and that you don't burn yourself. Ideally you would have special gloves or at least a towel or rags in that situation. If there is any question that there is an actual fire, it is best to not open the hood as mentioned. It is possible that your fan belt is broken or that a radiator hose has leaked, come loose or even disintegrated, or your radiator has a leak and you have lost all your coolant. In the case of a radiator leak, you may be able to add enough water or coolant to drive to a service station or mechanic if it is not too far away, or you may be one of the few who carries tools and an extra fan belt and is equipped and knowledgeable in how to replace a broken fan belt or radiator hose or even handle a radiator leak. **Even if you aren't capable of doing that, it is a good idea to keep an extra fan belt in the trunk.**

If you are a truck driver with special training in carrying potentially hazardous loads, there may be different instructions and indications for your proper action, which may differ from what is said in this context.

ROLLOVERS

Rollovers are dangerous accidents that have a higher fatality rate than other types of crashes. They are more common in SUVs, vans, and trucks because of the higher center of gravity. Rollover crashes account for approximately 1/3 of passenger vehicle fatalities.

TRIPPED ROLLOVERS PROBABLY ACCOUNT FOR 95% of single vehicle rollovers. This happens when a vehicle leaves the road and slides sideways, striking an object such as a curb or guard rail. Pavement surface irregularities, snow banks and other objects can cause a vehicle to roll over. A vehicle traveling forward, typically at a high speed, that has one side of the vehicle riding up on an object, such as a guard rail, can roll over.

Tripping can also occur on severe slopes and off road situations. If an incline slope is too steep to keep the vehicle upright, it can topple over. Drivers who take four wheel drive vehicles off-road have to be very aware of this.

Electronic stability control is helpful in many situations to help drivers stay on the road particularly when taking a curve at too great a speed. In 2010, one well known popular luxury car was having difficulties with electronic stability control. Unfortunately, the more sophisticated the car becomes, the more things can go wrong. Instead of relying on computers and automation, which can be helpful, it is still recommended that drivers also exercise caution, focus, judgment, and other good driving practices. Ejection from the vehicle is often associated with fatalities. Always have your seatbelt buckled.

Un-tripped rollovers are less common and occur mostly with top heavy vehicles. They usually occur during high speed collision avoidance maneuvers.

18-wheel semi-tractor-trailers and other large trucks often roll over, especially on slippery surfaces when they are cut off too quickly by passing cars or other trucks, causing them to brake or swerve suddenly. Shifting of a load can also be a factor.

STUCK GAS PEDAL

A stuck gas pedal can cause unintended acceleration. When you realize that you are experiencing a sudden unintended acceleration, put the car into neutral immediately, or if it is a manual transmission, put the clutch in and then put the car in neutral, brake and pull over to the side.

U NFORTUNATELY, SUDDEN UNINTENDED ACCELERATION HAS HAPPENED in many makes of cars, some more than others. Toyota had a major problem with this in 2009. When unintended acceleration happens, you usually will be very aware of it, and hopefully you will have enough time and distance from the traffic in front of you to react before you strike something. If your car has a tachometer, you may notice it going higher than usual. Don't waste time looking at it.

Practice putting your car into neutral in a safe place, such as an empty parking lot or an empty street, so that you are comfortable with the positions and the action necessary. Nowadays many cars are made with brake overrides, and many cars are being retrofitted with this. This means that if you brake hard, even if the accelerator is stuck or being pressed upon, the fuel line will be shut off. Some claim that in present cars, with a stuck accelerator, braking would still stop the car in only a slightly greater distance than if the gas pedal was not stuck. I don't think that's necessarily true, and you need to know how to get the car into neutral quickly. If you have the car in neutral, you can try tapping the gas pedal several times, but you are more likely to be successful if you can hook your toe under the gas pedal and flip it up.

If you initially can't get the car into neutral, then you may have to turn the engine off, i.e. to the accessory location, and not completely off.

Although you will lose the power assist for steering and braking, that's better then turning the ignition key all the way off, such as you would do when removing the key, since that will often lock up the steering. If your car works off of a start/stop button, you may have to push and hold the off switch (button) on the dash several seconds to turn off the engine. Newer cars may do this much quicker. If you have a push start/stop push button, you might want to push it (or hold it in if necessary), to see how long it takes to turn off the motor. You may lose power steering and power brake assist until you restart the motor, which is usually possible only in park.

Once you are off the road and onto the shoulder or another safe place, you should put your emergency flashers on if you have not already done so.

> **This actually happened to me in 2010 and fortunately, I knew exactly what to do. Being far enough behind the car in front of you gives you a little extra time.**

You can get out of the car, preferably on the passenger (non-traffic) side and you can reach down and raise the gas pedal with your hand, whether inside or outside of the car. If you reach down and raise the pedal with your hand while still driving, you usually will lose visual control and steering of the car and will probably endanger yourself even more. While a passenger in the front seat might be able to unstick the gas pedal, even that could be unsafe. Following the above advice, i.e. putting the car in neutral, and braking, or putting the clutch in if it is a manual transmission, and then putting the car in neutral, is the best approach, in my opinion.

Sudden unintended acceleration has been felt to be due to improper floor mats pressing on the gas pedal, true sticking of the gas pedal, and in some instances it has been speculated that there has been a computer malfunction. You need to take the car into the dealer as soon as possible to have this fixed. In some instances, you may even need to have the car towed. Always watch for recalls in regards to the above.

SUMMARY: If you have unintended acceleration, get the gear into neutral or put in the clutch if it is a manual transmission, pull off the road safely and if you are not able to get the car into neutral, turn the engine off by turning the key to the accessory position so that you will not lock up the steering, even though you may lose power steering and power assist braking. If you need to push on a start/stop button to turn off the engine, make sure you are familiar with how long it takes to do this in your car.

WHAT TO DO IN CASE
OF AN ACCIDENT

FIRST OF ALL, NEVER LEAVE THE scene. The legal penalties for that are extreme, and obviously you yourself would not want to be the victim of a hit and run driver, whether you were a pedestrian, or in your car.

> You should pull over, turn off your engine, put on your emergency flashers, and exit your car carefully, unless for some reason you feel your safety or even your life is in danger. If so, roll up your windows and lock your doors and call 9-1-1. There could be situations where even those actions may not insure your safety. You may have to use judgment, and even leave the scene, especially if you suspect the accident was staged to commit a crime, or an uncontrollable mob is attacking your car. If that occurs, report this immediately to the police at 9-1-1.

Under more usual circumstances, check to see if anyone in your car or in the other car or cars, or any pedestrians are injured. If they are, call 9-1-1 and then give necessary first aid depending upon your training. It is best not to move injured persons, but sometimes a fire and possible imminent explosion will necessitate that risk.

Generally speaking, an injured person should be covered with a coat or blanket since that will help prevent shock. Injured persons should lie down, safely away from traffic. Bleeding should be stopped, and any other first aid measures that you are trained in and comfortable with should be carefully and skillfully applied.

If you happen to have On-Star, activated by air bag deployment, this automatically notifies authorities and also gives your location. Some

Smartphones will have GPS and can function in this regard. If you don't have On-Star or any other device, it is important to have some idea where your location is, even if you only know which highway you are on, or which towns are near, or approximately where you are and in which direction you are traveling. That is something that is overlooked by most drivers until they get into a situation and then they realize they may not know their exact or even their approximate location.

In accidents where no one is injured, drivers still need to share information about their name, insurance company, license plate, driver's license, make, model, color, and year of involved cars. It is also important to either get the names and phone numbers of witnesses, or if they are reluctant to give out that information, to give them your phone number so that they could call you if they are so inclined.

Depending upon the state you live in and the amount of damage, it is important to report an accident, even without injuries, within a certain time-frame, to the police station in the jurisdiction in which the accident occurred. In some localities, this could be within 30 minutes, and in other cases it could be within several days. Also, there is often a state requirement as well for reporting an accident, and again this varies according to the state and the amount of damage. Always, if there is an injury, it is important to file a report with the state and the local jurisdiction. You should notify your insurance company. If the other driver was at fault and the other insurance company pays, even if you have notified your insurance company as a courtesy, they ordinarily will not count this against you. Check with your insurance company, since there may be limits or percentage of fault which could affect the above.

If no one is injured, and if you are obstructing traffic, if you are safely able to do so, it is a good idea to take a picture with a cell phone, or with a camera that you might have on your person or in the glove compartment, and then, if the car or cars are drivable, move them to a safer place (out of the traffic lanes) to allow drivers to exchange information and the traffic to pass. This is posted as a state law on some Chicago area toll roads. If there is damage, it is important to ask the police to respond unless weather or other conditions have created a situation where they have advised otherwise. In instances of severe weather, such as snow or ice storms, or blizzards, many states, because of the very bad weather (and the law authorities being too occupied with more serious incidents to respond), will request that information be exchanged and both parties report the accident within a set period of time. In other words, law enforcement may not respond to the site of an accident where no one is injured and the cars are drivable, under extremely adverse weather conditions.

If your car needs to be towed, the police will usually ask you if you have a particular towing service to contact, and if not, they will have towing companies that they can work with. If you are in your neighborhood, usually you will know of a reputable car repair shop that will often tow, or you could have the car towed to that facility.

You may have to notify relatives of your need to be picked up, and that could be at the scene of the accident or the local police station or the repair shop. The police are not obligated to give you a ride, but usually they will bring you to the police station or your home if nearby.

Thinking about all of the above, I'm hoping that the readers of this book will understand why it is so important to do everything they can to avoid being involved in an accident.

If you are a woman and bumped from behind, and two men get out of the car that hit you, you might be wise to keep your windows closed and your doors locked. You can call 9-1-1 and ask for assistance if you feel it was intentional or you are in danger. If not boxed in, you might choose to drive to a nearby police station or well lit gas station, in which case you should also keep your emergency flashers on. Most rear-enders are legitimate, but be aware of the rare exceptions, especially in remote areas.

Have a card showing who should be notified in case of an emergency and their home, work, and cell phone numbers, and a second back up. Also include any medical condition, for EMTs (Paramedics). I think it is a good idea to not only have it in the glove compartment (except for the problems that could arise if the car is stolen or broken into), but also on your person, such as in a pocket or purse, should you be involved in an accident and a card not be accessible from the glove compartment.

In July of 2009, the IL Secretary of State's office established an Emergency Contact Database. This allows Illinois residents who hold a driver's license or ID card to voluntarily register emergency contact information to be used should the registrant be involved in a crash or become incapacitated in some way. Other states may have also done this.

ACCIDENTS - ON THE SIDE OF, OR ON THE ROAD

IT CAN BE DISTRACTING, AND EVEN upsetting, when you see an accident on the side of the road. It is important to have some plan as to how to react.

There is a certain inherent danger of being the first on the scene, although you could be a life saver. The danger is that this could be a set-up. There are criminals with bad intentions who may be staging an accident to lure a passerby so they can hijack their car, rob them, or even worse. If you are alone and you are the first one there, you may be very vulnerable. The odds are that it is a real accident, but be cautious. The driver involved could be unstable or intoxicated and may rarely even become violent.

If someone needs to be pulled out of a wreckage of a car that is on fire, you might save a life and be a hero. This is a judgment call and much of it depends on what risk you are willing to take, and how you would want them to react to you, if you were the accident victim.

> If there is any question, particularly if you are alone, especially if you are a woman and again especially if it is a remote location, it is best that you go down the road a bit, stop, and call 9-1-1 to report an accident. Once the authorities are on the scene, then you can also help if needed.

On the other hand, if you come across an accident where there are already a number of cars stopped, and a number of people seem to be trying to help the victims of the accident, then that by itself suggests a safer circumstance for you to become involved in, if that is your choice. If there are no police, fire or ambulance personnel on the scene, you should call 9-1-1 again to be certain that they have been alerted.

If you do encounter an injured person in a car, you should try to stop the bleeding, and if there is a fire, you may need to move the trapped person, and that is hazardous because there could be an injury to the spinal cord. On the other hand, *if* the fire looks like it could lead to the death of the car occupant or occupants, and/or an explosion, then it is possible that the risk of injuring them further may be a reasonable one to take under the circumstance.

If there is *no fire*, and there is *no bleeding* that needs to be stopped, then probably you could wait until trained personnel arrive, unless cardiac resuscitation or other action is indicated.

Good Samaritan laws in many states offer legal immunity to those who offer assistance, especially if the assistance is reasonably rendered.

TRAFFIC STOPS BY POLICE OFFICERS

If you are pulled over for speeding, or for that matter any other reason, (this advice comes from State Troopers) pull over as soon as possible even if you think you might not be the one that the police car is trying to stop. Show that you have the proper respect for the emergency vehicle's right-of-way, and pulling over doesn't necessarily mean to the officer that you are admitting guilt. You would pull over even if you think the police officer was trying to stop a car behind or in front of you. Always pull over to the right side of the roadway on divided highways. Signal and safely move over to the far right lane and onto the shoulder, if necessary. When you come to a complete stop, choose a section of the roadway that has a full shoulder, without guardrails or fencing, if possible.

PULLING OVER ON THE LEFT MAY obstruct traffic, and pulling over to the left next to a guardrail, fence or concrete barrier may make it difficult for the officer to safely approach your car. If you are near a well-lit parking lot or easily accessible side street, you could pull into that area to make it safer for the police officer, i.e. to get away from heavy traffic. You should put on your emergency flashers and go slowly so the police officer knows your intentions.

Know where your paperwork is, i.e. your vehicle registration if needed for out of state travel, and especially your proof of insurance and your drivers license.

If you are not well organized and you keep the officer waiting while you dig through your possessions trying to find the proper papers and documentation, the officer might be less likely to sympathize with your cause. It may take the officer a few minutes to run your license plate to be sure you are not driving a stolen vehicle and that you are not a wanted felon or there is a warrant for your arrest. In case any of this applies, there may be a further delay, waiting for requested back up.

> **Make the officer feel safe, turn on your dome light at night, always keep your hands in plain sight, don't make any sudden movements, and roll your window all the way down.**

Stay in your car unless requested by the officer to exit, use common sense, and again don't put the officer in an uncomfortable situation. Let the officer speak first. Don't blurt out things that could incriminate you. Keep calm, even if you are upset about being stopped. Don't volunteer information such as how fast you thought you were going. The officer might not be pulling you over for what you think he or she is pulling you over for. Let the officer speak to you first. React courteously and you may have a greater chance of going on your way without receiving a ticket.

Don't argue with a policeman. Challenging a police officer is not in your, or their best interest. If you are issued a ticket and wish to contest it, set a date for court.

The Illinois Rules of the Road reminds drivers that if they wish to offer an explanation of their circumstances when stopped, do so before the officer returns to his or her vehicle. The officer cannot void the ticket once it has been written. Cooperate during the incident even if you believe you have not committed an offense. If you believe you have been treated unfairly, present your case in traffic court and not to the officer along the roadway. You are to be treated with dignity and respect by the officer. If you believe that the officer has acted inappropriately during a traffic stop or other encounter, you should report that conduct as soon as possible to the officer's superiors. Officers are required to provide their names and badge numbers upon request. A written ticket will contain the name of the officer.

If you are stopped by a uniformed police officer in a standard police car, stay in your car. If it is an unmarked car and/or you have any reason to be concerned that this may be someone impersonating a police officer, then you can, by law, proceed to the nearest police station, gas station or well lit parking lot. Again in that case, you should put your flashers on and go slowly so that the following officer knows that you are doing that. You can also honk your horn to attract attention if you feel you are in danger. In many areas you can call 9-1-1 to confirm that unmarked cars are in the area and give other information to the operator.

> **Particularly if you are a woman, and if stopped by a marked or especially an unmarked police car, and you question whether it is a legitimate policeman or plain clothes policeman, remember that it could be a carjacker, another type of criminal, or even a rapist. You can call the emergency number 9-1-1, and ask not only if there are unmarked cars in the area, but also if they will send a back up squad to check it out. Ask the 9-1-1 operator to stay on the line until the back up arrives. Again, in this situation, if you feel threatened, put your flashers on to show that you are aware, and slowly proceed to a well lit area, gas station or preferably a police or fire station. In some municipalities, unmarked police cars will not make routine traffic stops at night. Check with your police department.**

CARJACKING

CARJACKING IS WHEN SOMEONE, USUALLY WITH a weapon, forcibly takes your car. If you are in your car and someone comes up to it with questionable or obvious evil intention, if your door is locked and your window is closed, and your motor is running and your car is in gear, and you have space in front of or behind you, you can use your car as a weapon to get away, even dragging the person if they stick their hand through an open window or if they have broken the window. Remember when stopping your car in traffic, leave enough space in front of you so that you can pull around the car in front of you if necessary, if that space is open.

Carjacking and abduction continue to be a threat to all drivers. This crime can occur anywhere, such as when a person is approaching their vehicle in a parking lot, or anywhere else, day or night, or even moving slowly through heavy traffic.

Sometimes carjackers kidnap the driver, or they may force the driver from the car and drive off with other occupants, including children, still inside the car. This is a good reason to not refuel with children in the car, and also it is a good reason to constantly be focused and alert. There are tens of thousands of carjackings in the United States each year. **When loading groceries or other items into your car, put them in the car first and *children last*. *Carjackings*** often occur close to the victim's home, sometimes even within the victim's own garage. Carjackers depend on the element of surprise and that is why it is so important when you are entering or exiting your car to be very alert, focused, and careful.

In some instances, drivers and/or their passengers may be assaulted, and in these instances, the perpetrator is not interested in the car or the keys, but rather rape or robbery. Purse thefts are common in attacks on drivers in cars. As with most random crimes, the perpetrators will often choose a victim who seems to be timid or not concentrating, or even somewhat lackadaisical. Someone who appears confident is less likely to be the victim of a violent crime, although there is no guarantee in that regard.

Any confrontation with a carjacker or any attacker is potentially dangerous and the intended victim should realize that the attacker may be on drugs, may be desperate, may be armed, and may be capable of doing anything.

Starting from when you go to your garage, whether in a condominium, apartment building, whether the parking is inside or outside, or in an office building or any other parking situation, or even your own driveway or garage, be alert for any suspicious circumstances, and if there are any, turn around and go back and notify security or the police.

Have your key out, and if possible open the car door with your remote as you approach it. Know where the panic button is on the remote so that if you do sense danger, you can at least make considerable noise by holding the button down to attract attention. If you are walking to your car in a parking lot, observe the nearby vehicles, and if there is a van or truck, particularly with a male on the passenger side immediately next to your car, be suspicious and seek the help of security personnel.

When approaching your car, it is easier to look under a high vehicle such as an SUV, pickup truck, or a van, from a distance, than it is to do this when you are up close. Some attackers and carjackers have actually hidden under vehicles. Along those lines, it is important to park in well lit, busy spaces, rather than isolated, dimly lit, and remote areas of a parking lot.

If you keep your car in an attached garage, open the garage door only after you've gotten into, and locked your car, and then start the car *after* you open the garage door. If you have a garage which is not attached, you will have to be even more alert for suspicious circumstances.

Whether approaching a car, or already in the car, or exiting and leaving your car, every car jacking or abduction or assault situation is different, and the response could be different from person-to-person and situation-to-situation.

As an example, if you are threatened from a distance, most people would initially yell or scream and start to run away. If the attacker starts to chase you, you might decide to throw your keys away from you and in the opposite direction that you are running, so that the attacker would have to either stop or turn around to go back to get the keys. If you don't throw your keys, or if they are separate from the key fob, remember to use the panic button on the key fob, if the carjacker continues to follow you. This example applies to an announced carjacking. There is a risk that setting off the car alarm will anger the potential carjacker, making him less likely to go back to a car with an alarm on, and perhaps more likely to attack you.

Some authorities on crime suggest that if a carjacker or attacker has a gun and orders you out of the car, it is probably a good idea to follow their instructions, unless they ask you to get into the trunk. There are a number of authorities who say that you should never get into a trunk, and instead you should run away in a weaving (zig-zag) fashion. The thinking is that if an attacker does shoot, they are not likely to hit you, and if they do, it is not likely to be fatal. Personally I would not depend on their intention nor their presumed inaccuracy, since people have been fatally shot resisting, even running away from carjackers.

There are people who have been forced into a trunk who have survived, and there are others who have perished in the trunk, either because of the weather, or because of criminal action, and even medical conditions, and there are drivers who have been killed because they resisted. Not only are there trunk release straps in modern cars, but also some people put into trunks have been able to use their cell phone to summon help. Hopefully the reader will never be in this situation, but it is a good idea to think of what your likely reaction would be, even though circumstances may change what you thought you would do. There is a certain risk in any action you take, as well as any inaction (lack of taking an action). If you choose to try to escape from a trunk, it is best for the car to be slowly moving and in an area where there are many people.

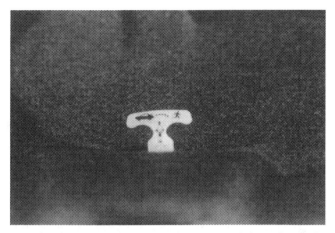

A trunk release strap allows opening the trunk from the inside.

Although most drivers obviously won't ever be faced with this situation, it is still a good idea to have thought through your reaction if in fact you are the exception that is confronted. If you need to, you should have help in determining whether the truck release strap will work if the trunk is locked and you may find this in your manual or the dealer may help you with this.

If your car is hijacked, i.e. you are carjacked, you should alert the authorities as soon as possible so that they can both look for your car and the carjacker. If there is a child or children in the car, the police will make an incredible effort to quickly locate the car to save the child or children. In most instances, carjackers have not harmed children who were in the car. Again that's another reason to be alert and cautious and particularly to not refuel with small children in the car, if you can avoid it. It is also another reason to park only in well lit places close to the entrance or exit to where you are going, rather than in remote isolated areas.

You have to be alert when you are approaching your car, driving, and exiting and leaving a car. As you approach your car, always look for abductors *inside* your car, particularly noticing any jimmied door or broken window. Always lock your car doors and keep your windows closed when you leave your car. It is best to lock your car with the button on the car door, since using the key fob makes it easier for someone to highjack the code and to enter your car.

Once you are in your car, and the doors are locked and the windows are closed, starting the engine gives you an additional tool for a safe exit.

Some people suggest backing into a parking space so it will be easier to leave going forward. Actually, the gear ratio of backing up is very powerful, and if you are a reasonably good driver, you may be able to create sufficient disruption to the attacker's intention, as you escape an attacker by backing up.

If you are surprised as you open your car door and the attacker has a knife, and forces you to drive, you might decide to obey, that is until the first opportunity to purposely wreck the car by turning the attacker's side of the car into a pole or building and then immediately jumping out of the car. Obviously there is a risk in this action as there is in not taking any action. If the carjacker is driving and you are sitting in the passenger seat, it would be harder to do this, but then it also might be harder for them to use their weapon.

The difficulty in all of this discussion is that drivers have survived by complying, and others have perished. Some drivers have survived by taking forceful action, and some in doing that, have been injured or killed. As a general rule, I would not argue with a person armed with a gun or a knife who was standing close to me. I would comply, ordinarily, but again circumstances may dictate otherwise.

Remember that people can't be replaced, but cars can be.

Most carjacking and assaults occur in parking lots, such as those connected to shopping centers, convenience stores, banks, motels, hotels, and restaurants. Gas stations are another place where you have to be very alert. ATM locations may be especially tempting to a carjacker or a robber. As mentioned, carjacking can occur in your parking space in your neighborhood, in your driveway, even in your garage.

If there is mud, or snow in the winter, watch for fresh footprints that might suggest someone is already planning to victimize you or your car.

Some suggest carrying a whistle because it creates substantial noise with a fairly small effort. Perhaps the panic button on your remote car key fob can accomplish the same result, or even better.

Sometimes carjackers will work in pairs, i.e. two to a car and they will follow you and wait for a somewhat secluded area before attacking. They also might have two cars working in tandem. They might bump your car and gesture for you to pull over. If you are at all suspicious, immediately call 9-1-1 and *don't stop*, especially in a deserted or remote area, put your flashers on and drive to a safe place, i.e. a well lit and busy filling station or police station or fire station. You might even honk your horn as you are doing this to attract attention. Ordinarily your key fobs panic button will not sound an alarm if the car is running. Remember the most danger is in a secluded place that would not provide any witnesses. If in fact it was a legitimate accident, you need to tell the policeman investigating, that you were fleeing a possible carjacker.

When our kids were little, during the 1970s, when things were a little tense, we had special phrases such as "hit the deck" and "take cover." They were told that if they heard those commands they should not ask any questions, as children are prone to do, but rather to take cover (hide behind something substantial).

If you are picking up a child at school, it is a good idea to keep your doors locked and your windows up and if for some reason you are the victim of an attack, prepare your child with a special phrase such as "Do you have your homework?" and you can discuss that with your child as to what might be appropriate. This would alert the child that they need to run and get help. It would also remove the child from the dangerous zone. Children should memorize the license plate and description of their car so that they can give this to authorities.

Carry a pen and notebook for jotting down license numbers and descriptions of suspects and their vehicles, or use a recording device for that purpose.

There is no way to be 100% safe, but the more one has thought through their potential actions in an unlikely situation, the more likely there will be a successful outcome.

It is best to not keep your car or office keys on the same key ring that you have your car keys on, but if your house or office keys are taken from you, then you should alert the police as soon as possible, and you should also have your locks changed immediately.

The above is not intended to create excessive worrying and paranoia, but is intended to emphasize that alert and focused attention in thinking through a situation is a sensible effort to avoid being a victim.

SUMMARY: As in so many chapters, subchapters and sections of *Sane Driving in a Mad World*, the summary is unrealistic because everything in the content of the chapter is important and drivers are advised to read the entire text carefully.

CHARITABLE DONATIONS BEING SOLICITED AT INTERSECTIONS WITH TRAFFIC LIGHTS

PERSONALLY I'VE ALWAYS FELT THAT CHARITABLE donations shouldn't be solicited at intersections. On the other hand, when I'm able, I try to support many worthy organizations.

Even though soliciting at intersections with traffic lights seem to be the best way for many organizations to raise money, I believe it is dangerous for those soliciting, and it often inconveniences drivers. I have seen a situation where there was much snow, and a solicitor was perched on a narrow ledge of snow and ice as cars were sliding within inches of the solicitor in a left turn lane. I still think it is dangerous for solicitors, but on the other hand, if traffic has come to a stop and you are waiting for the light to change, and you can easily make a contribution that you want to, without inconveniencing the drivers behind you, then that's your choice and it is reasonable.

If you are getting ready to start or you are not intending to contribute, when a solicitor comes up to your car, you can just shake your head to indicate "no" politely. They are used to that, and if they are pushy, you don't have to respond. Ordinarily they won't be.

When the light has changed to green or an arrow, solicitors are supposed to not be soliciting at that point so that they don't hinder the progression of the cars through the light or the arrow. I have witnessed a number of violations of the above policy. I have read about people legitimately soliciting at busy intersections, who were in fact injured. I have witnessed solicitors standing on the line separating lanes during a heavy rain, when vision was difficult.

FUNERAL PROCESSIONS

I'VE ALWAYS BEEN RESPECTFUL OF AND honored the sanctity of a funeral procession in spite of the occasional temporary inconvenience. On the other hand, I've often thought that it would be just as appropriate if they would give directions to the mourners who wanted to go from the funeral home to the cemetery. In that situation, probably many people would get lost, and there is some comfort (consolation) when mourners are part of a group. In some situations, the cemetery has a chapel right on the grounds, so that eliminates any problems in this area. Also, some funerals are held at the graveside.

It is important to not pull into a funeral procession unless you are really a part of it. You need to let all the cars that are designated to be in the funeral procession go by before you cross an intersection or pull out. If you are in a left turn lane and the procession crosses in front of you to the left, you might decide to take an alternate route if you can safely pull out of the left turn lane in order to go straight or even to turn right. If you are close to your destination and in the right lane, you might especially decide to turn right and pursue an alternate route.

If you see cars going through a red light and you wonder from a distance what is going on, look to see if they don't have a funeral procession marker on them, or their flashers or flag or something else designating that they are in a funeral procession, because that happens frequently, and you do need to extend courtesy and respect to those cars in that situation, and it is the law.

GPS UNITS

While GPS is usually a welcome convenience, drivers using them have sometimes ended up lost in remote locations. They're less likely to do that if the software is updated every several years. I remember having one in a rental car in Boston some 14 years ago, and if I had blindly followed the directions given, I would have ended up in the Boston Harbor, because of construction closing some roads. In general, they can be another distraction if addresses and other inputs are not entered before you start the car, or while you are stopped, or by a passenger. Some newer units allow voice input.

One of the main advantages of a portable GPS is that if you are in a rental car in a distant unfamiliar location, it can be very helpful to have a GPS. While rental cars are available with this, it may be advantageous if you have your own and are more familiar with its programming.

> One of the problems that I have seen with GPS units is that they don't always direct you by the most efficient or even the shortest route, and sometimes definitely not by the safest route. In general, staying on freeways and expressway is safer than going through unfamiliar neighborhoods, and a GPS generally doesn't take this into account, although some offer you choices, i.e. shortest distance versus shortest time, or other options. Unfortunately, some cars on expressways have been random targets of shooters. Be alert even on freeways and expressways.

I've found that having a compass in a car, one which might be integrated into the rear view mirror, is very helpful, although not as distinctly helpful as a GPS. A GPS should tell you that you are approaching a certain street in so many feet and you need to turn left (in so many feet, or whatever measurement is appropriate), rather than just saying turn right or turn left at such and such a street (in which case you have to be looking for street signs).

Some GPS units have features such as real time traffic reporting as well as voice command capability. A portable unit should be securely mounted, preferably on the dash, to prevent possible injury in an accident, making sure that it is out of the path of an air bag deployment. It is also important to hide it or take it with you when you leave the car.

If a portable GPS loses its battery charge, you should ordinarily have a cord which can connect to a power outlet.

If you get out of your car to do some hiking, or bushwhacking or trail exploring, a hand held GPS can help you to follow your trail back to your car, or even share coordinates in an emergency, helping searchers find you if you are lost.

I have had the experience of a portable GPS telling me to turn left directly into the middle of a cornfield. If the GPS voice is not loud, turn off the radio and request conversation to stop when directions are given.

In 2010, a hiker sued a major computer map producing company. She was directed to a rural highway with no sidewalk, walking path, or shoulder, and was struck and injured by a car. A suitable warning that there may not be a shoulder or walking path on all routes would ordinarily appear on a computer, but not on a cell phone, PDR, or other hand held device, at the time.

A driver was killed when directed by a GPS onto a closed road leading to a drop off. If there are barriers or signs, follow their directions rather than the GPS.

Many cell phones now incorporate GPS, which is both convenient and helpful. While a GPS may seem to be directing you in a roundabout way, even counterintuitive to what you suspect may be a better route, it may be aware of construction or other unusual delays by the more conventional route.

DIRECTIONS (INCLUDING FOLLOWING A FRIEND'S CAR)

WHEN YOU GIVE DIRECTIONS TO SOMEONE, try to use landmarks and also distances, i.e. turn right at the Shell Station, go two miles, turn left at the stop light where there is a McDonald's on the far left corner, etc. If you are using MapQuest or Google, it is a good idea to write directions in large print on either a card or full sheet, so that if you or a passenger has to look at it, it is easy to see with a minimum amount of distraction. It is much better to stop in a safe place to look at directions, than it is to try to read while driving.

It is important to not follow friends since that encourages drivers to go through yellow or red lights and in general is just not a safe way to drive. It is much better to give explicit directions, and every driver should have a pen or pencil and paper in their glove compartment or console for such purposes. With GPS so readily available, the above may be less relevant.

MOUNTAIN DRIVING

For steep hills or mountain driving, both going up and down, use lower gears to take the stress off the engine going uphill and the stress off the regular brakes going downhill. Some of the above depends on the severity of the grade, but often there may be signs to indicate that you should shift to a lower gear. At higher speeds, down-shifting in stages, especially with automatic transmissions, is less likely to damage the car, or cause a skid on slippery surfaces.

IN A REALLY WINDING MOUNTAIN ROAD with steep drop offs and hairpin curves, obviously you want to drive cautiously and slowly, and you'll probably often be in a lower gear depending upon the road and the incline, and possibly the pace of the traffic ahead of you.

If you are sightseeing in your own car or a rental car, don't stop suddenly to view the scenery, only stop where there are pull-off areas that are designed for sightseeing, and usually they are indicated by signs several hundred feet before the viewing area. In the mountains, if you stop, someone who is used to the roads might come around a mountain very fast, and if you are stopped in the middle of the road, this could result in a crash or even a car running off of, or into the mountain.

"Black ice" can be on the shady side of a mountain, or even the shady side of a hill, or even on level roads. Be aware, if you are coming from the sun into the shade, if it is cold and there has been ice or snow, or even fog, because you could hit black ice. You would need to adjust your speed accordingly, anticipating this. If you skid on black ice, take your foot off of the gas, don't brake (it won't help), and don't turn the steering wheel. Avoidance where possible is best.

Working two summers in the Colorado Mountains while a pre-medical and medical student, always on Mondays there would be new sightings of cars that had gone off the road, and tumbled down the mountain side, usually for hundreds of feet. Speed and alcohol, and likely lack of familiarity with the road may have contributed.

Make sure the front windshield and the back window, and the side windows and mirrors are free of dirt, snow and ice.

> **If you encounter a car coming in the opposite direction in a narrow area where there is only room for one car, the car going *uphill* should *stop* and give the *right of way* to the car going *downhill*.**

Always remember that when you are driving in the mountains at certain times of the year there can be the danger of an avalanche, rock or mud slide. Watch for signs and listen to radio reports. If you are caught in an avalanche, leave your lights on if they work, and turn your motor off to avoid carbon monoxide poisoning. You may be able to use your cell phone to call for help. See section on Avalanches and refer to the book called "110 Car and Driving Emergencies" by James Joseph (Lyons Press or Amazon).

If you can see some sunlight coming through the snow, you may not be that deep. Honk your horn to attract the attention of rescuers.

See the Chapter on braking, for advice on losing brakes in the mountains.

DRIVING SCHOOLS

THERE ARE ADVERTISEMENTS IN MANY LOCAL newspapers about driving schools and some are particularly aimed at teenagers and others are aimed at older drivers. Older drivers do have access to AARP's refresher courses. In some areas there may be a program called "Alive at 25" which is taught to teenagers by experienced police officers with the goal that they will not become a victim, because they will learn better driving safety habits and attitudes. Most young drivers will have attended driver education classes at school and will have certificates to show successful completion.

There are a number of private certified driving schools located throughout the country. For those who don't have access to other means of learning to drive, these schools can be very useful. Ask to see proof of certification of the school. There are some driving schools, particularly in the western states that can actually reproduce various hazardous road and weather conditions. These schools can teach higher levels of defensive driving under adverse conditions, even going so far as to teach drivers how to evade kidnappers and attacks by terrorists. Usually these schools are quite expensive and one could go onto the Internet if one is interested in driving schools of this nature in or outside their area.

There are some that last one day and other's last several days. Bob Bondurant is the name most of us associate with professional driving schools, although there are others. Some of these courses are designed to help young drivers, as well as mature and older drivers, how to handle a car in a skid, and also to learn how to make evasive maneuvers to avoid a crash.

"Top Driver" has a good reputation. They have 31 locations in Illinois including a number in Chicago and Suburbs, and they do have online driver education as well. They also have 33 locations in Ohio, as well as an online instruction. They do have two locations in Michigan and again Topdriver.com would help the driver access that. A-Adams School of Driving has a good reputation in the Chicago and North Suburban area and also in several other Midwestern locales.

Locally, family members have been pleased with All Suburban Driving School, and New Concept Driving School, both in Grayslake, Illinois.

POTPOURRI (MISCELLANEOUS)

Blind Pedestrians

OFTEN THERE ARE MARKERS WHERE BLIND pedestrians might be crossing, and one should slow down and be cautious. If you see someone with a seeing eye dog, and that's usually fairly easy to recognize, not so much by the type of dog, as much as by the harness and the way they are moving, then certainly you should slow down and yield the right of way. A blind person might have a white cane, with or without a red tip. Sometimes they will have dark glasses even when the sun isn't shining, including at night.

> Blind persons rely to a large extent on hearing, and if you happen to have a hybrid or electric car, it may be so quiet at times that this will present a problem for them. If you drive a quieter car, you should be aware of this. Many newer hybrids and all-electric cars are adding some noise to make them safer for all pedestrians. Many visually impaired pedestrians are able to interpret the noise the tires make, especially starting and stopping.

> If there is a sign that indicates School for the Blind, or "Blind Crossing," you need to drive slowly in that area. A blind person at a crosswalk might take a step backward to show awareness of your presence, but this is no longer routinely taught. Thanks to Gregory Polman with the Chicago Lighthouse for reviewing and modifying the information on this subject. Gregory also pointed out that stopping before the crosswalk is an important way for drivers to aid visually impaired pedestrians. Seeing-eye service dogs are taught to go around the front of a protruding vehicle. Since they may have "intelligent disobedience" and choose otherwise, be alert to any pedestrian behind you, Gregory reminds all of us. Do not honk, unless trying to prevent an otherwise obvious disaster, since they have no way of knowing the meaning of the honk and it may frighten a blind pedestrian and/or their seeing-eye dog, if they have one.

Pedestrians

We are all pedestrians at times. Pedestrians are very vulnerable, and when a 3,000 lb. (or heavier) car meets a 150 lb. pedestrian, we all know who the loser is likely to be. Actually when that happens, both the driver of the car and the pedestrian are losers. Always, always give the right of way to a pedestrian. *Many pedestrians are handicapped, many are distracted, many simply don't obey the law.* Many jaywalk, often they walk along the right side of the road in the same direction as we as drivers are going, frequently at night even as they are wearing dark clothing. Just about any other conceivable act that you can imagine from a pedestrian, perhaps especially in parking lots and shopping centers, will necessitate your extreme caution and courtesy. The interest in PokemonGo, or other current rage may distract pedestrians or even drivers.

> **Especially in windy or bad weather, including snow and rain, pedestrians may have their vision obscured by clothing or by umbrellas or even by the wind and the snow itself. When there is snow and ice piled up on the sidewalk, frequently pedestrians will be in the street. We have to look at pedestrians pretty much as we look at bicycles, expect the unexpected, or as I have mentioned before, the unexpected actually becomes the expected. Truly when it comes to pedestrians, we need to be our brother's keeper.**

Pedestrians who are approaching crosswalks will often stop and indicate to drivers that they will wait for the driver, but if they have already arrived at the crosswalk, the law states that you must stop and allow them to cross. From a practical point of view, on a wide street, if pedestrians are going in the same direction that you are going, and you are turning left and there could be many seconds before they reach the lane that you are turning into, it seems reasonable that you could turn. It would be unreasonable and possibly dangerous to wait until the light has pretty much changed or until the pedestrian has finished crossing the street, since that might put you in the middle of an intersection blocking traffic or being in the path of an oncoming car. However, this may not be legal in your particular state. Obviously you have to use good judgment and do what would be legal and safe for the pedestrian. By the same token, if you are turning right or going through an intersection and a pedestrian has already gone out of your path and was headed for the other side of the street, you can slowly and safely proceed. **Check your state laws in this regard.** Remember if there is any doubt, always yield to a pedestrian.

As a pedestrian, be alert, you could be struck by a vehicle coming from any direction, even if you are on the sidewalk, or on a lawn, or at a bus stop or shelter.

Fumes from Outside the Vehicle

If you encounter a fire or some type of hazmat situation where there may be fumes, or smoke, sand, or dust outside the car, it is important to put your windows up and turn off any air conditioning or ventilation that might bring in outside air.

There may be serious polluters, i.e. cars or trucks whose exhausts are pouring dark colored obnoxious fumes. Besides reporting such events (and you probably shouldn't even get close enough to get their license number), the best thing is to stay far behind so that the fumes are dissipated. If you pass, do so quickly, with your input fans turned off, and your windows closed, so you would only be re-circulating inside air.

Fumes from Inside the Vehicle

Unfortunately, modern cars are often made with fabrics and dashboards that out-gas a number of chemicals, and this is especially true of new cars. You can probably get a new car to out-gas quicker if you turn the heat up high and have the windows open while you are driving, if you are able to. Some drivers are much more susceptible than others to the effect of chemical fumes from within the car. If your car sits outside in the sun, some recommend opening the door and/or windows to allow potentially harmful chemical fumes to escape, before turning on the air conditioner.

There are portable air filters that are designed to work inside cars. Unfortunately, they are usually not able to be safely attached to the vehicle to prevent them from becoming a dangerous moving object in a crash.

Cars Striking Buildings

In the Chicago area there are frequent instances of cars striking buildings, and it is likely that this can occur anywhere, perhaps more in densely populated areas. While usually on busy streets, this has also happened in residential areas where cars and even trucks and buses have struck homes, and occasionally businesses, and even houses of worship. While often only the driver is injured, in many instances occupants of a business and even a home are also injured or killed.

Speeding, alcohol, and drowsiness can all contribute to the above, as can automobile malfunction and medical conditions.

A frequent scenario is a driver parked up against a business in a parking lot, and the brakes are intended to be hit, but actually the gas is hit instead.

While often these accidents have involved older drivers, anyone can be at risk, depending upon the circumstances mentioned earlier.

If you are a customer in a business, particularly a restaurant, you might choose to be seated in the back, or far behind a very sturdy wall, particularly away from, rather than next to, windows that are facing or adjacent to a parking lot.

Expressway Driving or Four Lane Roads (Passing on the Right)

Although many years ago, it was illegal to pass on the right, generally there were only two lane highways at the time. With the advent of four-lane highways, passing on the left is still suggested, but unfortunately there are often cars in the left lane that are going slower and should move over, but don't. On a multi-lane highway or road, where there are at least two lanes in each direction, it is legal to pass on the right. Slow cars should be, if on the highway at all, in the right lane. The left lane or lanes should be for cars that intend to pass.

Hybrids and Electric Cars

For those who are concerned about long term effects of exposure to low frequency electromagnetic waves, they should probably arrange to measure the milligauss exposure particularly in the rear seat of a hybrid or electric car where the seat may be closest to the battery. In the few cars that I have measured, the levels were acceptable in the front seat but were a little high in the rear seat. If the car is used mainly for an adult commuter, i.e. one driver and one passenger in the front seat, then I wouldn't be too concerned. If, on the other hand, the car is used to transport small children in the rear seat much of the time, then one would have to decide which side of the unresolved argument one is on. My personal feeling in this still controversial subject is that prudent avoidance is a good choice. It may be that built in GPS and other electronics might also contribute to the electromagnetic field.

Gauss meters, i.e. devices to measure electromagnetic fields, can be obtained through the N.E.E.D.S. Catalog and through other sources such as the Internet. Google "gauss meters." The Tri-field meter is one of the least expensive and it correlates well with much more expensive professional models, in my experience.

Another issue with hybrids and electric cars may be the potential for electrocution and fire from the electrical system in case of a crash. Most first responders, i.e. police and firemen, are trained in how to avoid electrocution themselves and how to rescue passengers in that situation.

Going Under Bridges And Overpasses

Occasionally, an anti-social person or persons will throw objects off of overpasses or bridges, onto the road passing underneath. If these are rocks or any other solid objects, not only can they damage a car, but they can go through the windshield or sunroof, and even injure or kill the driver, or cause a severe, even fatal, accident.

If you encounter anything of this nature, if you are able to pull over to the side of the road and call authorities, this would be better than hoping it doesn't happen to your car. If you didn't realize that it was happening until you were already upon (under) it, after you've gone by, you should phone the authorities and ask them to quickly check it out, because it truly may be a matter of life and death for motorists behind you.

What To Do If You Suspect You Are Being Followed

If you think you are being followed by a car, make three right turns, but not into dark remote streets, and if the car is still behind you, it is likely, but still not for certain, that you are being followed. You might then make two more right turns and even a left turn. It could be someone who lives close to you, but if the car is still behind you, you should at that point, if you can, call 9-1-1 and identify your location and your car and the direction in which you are heading, and if you are able to, give any information about the car that you suspect is following you. Some experts advise making **sudden** left turns, and if the car following you does the same, then that's a tip off. Other experts advise just driving at normal speed so as not to alert the following car of your awareness.

If you are able to drive to a police station, a fire station, or a well lit and busy filling station or parking lot, or a busy truck stop, that may be all it takes to discourage the driver that is following you. Honk your horn to draw attention to your plight and that might also discourage someone who is following you.

If you are driving down your street and you suspect or realize that you are being followed, do not pull into your driveway. Keep driving to prevent being boxed in by the car behind you, or even attacked as you are getting out of your car in your driveway. You are likely to be much safer if you seek one of the safe havens mentioned above, and also you don't want the follower to know where you live.

If you do have a garage door opener, it is still a risky thing to try to pull into your garage, because someone who is intent on doing harm, and is following you closely, may be able to get in before you can close the garage door, in which case the situation can quickly become very dangerous.

The purpose of this chapter is not to make drivers paranoid, but simply to make drivers aware and alert and understand how to protect themselves in many situations, even those that hopefully won't arise.

What To Do If Your Car Breaks Down On The Road

If you have an AAA card or other roadside assistance card, you can call for help. They may ask on the phone if you need a tire changed, a battery jump, or a tow.

You should, particularly if it's an isolated area or nighttime, and especially if you are a woman, stay in your car. If someone comes up to help you, just say, "Please call for assistance" if you haven't yet been able to call for assistance. If you feel threatened by someone who comes up to help you, I recommend saying "No thanks, the police are on their way, and should be here any minute." Most drivers will have already called for assistance on their cell phone. Don't unlock the car and don't get out, and don't let anybody in. I think it is much easier for someone with evil intentions to break a window that is partially cracked open, but you may have to roll it down slightly, being careful because some newer car windows are difficult to lower just a slight amount, and you certainly don't want to open the window all the way.

It used to be recommended to have a big orange sign that says, "Call the Police" that you could put in your back window, but it is very difficult to actually get to the back seat unless you get out of your car to do this, and you may decide not to do that. This could also be put on the front windshield. You would probably need a small roll of scotch tape to keep it in place. Another problem with that is that it may signal to a "bad person" that you have not summoned help with a cell phone. If you have an aerial, you could put a white rag or handkerchief on it or you could even just leave part of the rag or handkerchief outside the driver's side window, which is also a signal that you need help. Fortunately, most people nowadays have a cell phone, so you won't see this often. If you encounter a car that is broken down, particularly if there is a person, especially a woman, alone, it is not a bad idea to call authorities even if the person may have already notified them.

Call for help early on and keep the car doors locked and the windows rolled up. Try to maintain your car so that you are less likely to be stuck because your car has broken down. Especially if you are a woman alone, you have to be very careful, but anyone can be victimized in this situation, although many drivers are often genuinely willing to help. Rarely, a driver who is trying to help is assaulted. The perpetrator may be on drugs or have a mental illness.

If you're traveling alone, especially if you are a woman, the daytime is likely to be preferable from a number of safety considerations. Also keeping a relatively full tank of gas is another important safety consideration.

Worst Days Including Times of Days for Crashes

Generally, Sundays can be bad, possibly because people have partied the night before or more likely because many drivers are out who wouldn't ordinarily be out, and they are somewhat unfocused. Although we refer to them as Sunday Drivers, most people who drive on Sunday are also driving on all of the other days. Statistically, Saturday is a more dangerous day to drive, followed by Sunday and then Friday. Certain days might present a greater danger from drivers who may be driving under the influence, and these could be the Fourth of July holiday or holiday weekend, New Years Eve or even the weekend, and St. Patrick's Day. On or close to Halloween, you have to be watchful for children trick-or-treating who may be wearing masks so that they can not see cars as well, and they may not have reflective costumes. Teenagers have more accidents between Memorial Day and Labor Day probably because they are out of school.

It is believed that there is increased alcohol consumption as families get together the night before Thanksgiving, requiring extra caution by drivers. Ordinarily for teenagers, and often for other drivers, the most dangerous time is 12:00 midnight to 3:00 a.m. In states where marijuana has been legalized, "driving under the influence" accidents have increased.

Many statistics have suggested that the hours after work, and the evenings, are the more hazardous, possibly because drivers are *tired* and hurrying to get home. I actually have listened to WBBM Radio in Chicago for many years, both in the morning and often during the evening rush hours, and there seems to be an abundance of crashes during the morning rush hours as well. Presumably drivers are trying to get to work on time and may or may not be well rested.

Possibly during any holiday weekend, the accident rate is up, and that is the reason that even before we had daytime running lights, many safety conscious drivers turned on their low beam headlights throughout the day during holidays and holiday weekends, still a good idea (even all of the time).

Ignition Key

Some automobile experts have recommended not carrying an excess of keys and other items on the key ring where you have your ignition key, since the extra weight could ruin the ignition switch, and that could be costly to fix. One major auto manufacturer (General Motors) has had a serious problem with ignition switches. They would turn off not only after being bumped, but also possibly from the weight of extra keys on the key ring, and then other functions such as the air bags and power steering would also become inoperative. A number of fatal crashes resulted and the auto maker did not issue a recall in a timely manner. In fact, they waited some ten years. Unfortunately, the replaced switches sometimes turned out to also be defective. This recall was in 2014 and 2015.

Curves

When coming around a sharp curve, always stay close to the right, and go slowly, especially if cars are parked on your right. Someone coming in the opposite direction may be "cutting the corner," or going over the yellow dividing lines. It seems to me that for blocks before a frequently encountered sharp curve, there are absolutely no cars, but when I get to the curve, there is often an opposing car. When turning right on red, or at a stop sign, if cars are coming from your left around a blind curve; or where you are turning left, the cars are coming around a curve from the right, use extreme caution, especially if the speed limit allows the cars to be traveling fairly fast at that point.

A car could be speeding in the opposite direction at a sharp turn.

Four Way Stop

When you stop at a four way stop sign, the tendency is to look to the right and to the left. The car to the right does have the right of way if it arrives at the same time. Sometimes it is hard to remember to look at the car that is coming from the opposite direction that you are traveling, and that car may be waiting to turn left, and may have been there before you, so check that and allow that car to turn, as proper courtesy demands.

Taxi

If you are taking a taxi, particularly at a later time of day, or in a questionable or unfamiliar area, and especially if you are a woman, it is my suggestion that when you get in, that you have either called a friend or home on your cell phone, or even just have the phone open and give the taxi cab company and number as well as your expected time of arrival and other pertinent information to a friend or just to a phone that you are holding, and say it so that the driver hears, to discourage criminal intent from the driver. Licensed professional drivers are carefully screened in most areas, and actually the driver is at much greater risk from passengers, but nevertheless this could be a simple crime deterrent even if you are speaking into a turned off phone.

Turn Signals

One of the things for all drivers, including senior drivers, to remember, is to turn off their turn signals after changing lanes or entering an expressway, or making a half turn into or from a diagonal street, or pulling out from a parallel parking space.

Hand Signals

Do not have one hand or one arm sticking out of the car, since in a crash you could lose an arm, besides having less control by having only one hand on the wheel. If you have to use hand signals because your turn signals are not working, remember to bring your arm back inside the car as soon as feasible. Know the proper hand signals for right turn, left turn, and slowing or stopping. See your state driver's manual or ask a trusted knowledgeable driver.

Sun Roofs

Sun roofs can be wonderful for a number of reasons, but there have been instances where attackers have threatened or attacked drivers and passengers with a knife or other weapon, through an open sun roof. It's usually not an issue at ordinary speeds, but if you are stopped or going slow in heavy traffic, you might want to be very aware of your surroundings and the opportunity that an open sun roof presents to an attacker, or to an object thrown from an overpass. When the sun roof is not open, keep the retractable cover under it closed, as a barrier to the rare spontaneous shattering of sun roofs.

Open Windows

Certain cars will shimmy and shake like they have a flat tire, similar to driving over a rough road, if you have one or more windows open. This can be a scary sensation going at expressway speeds. You should close your windows if you are going over 45 mph, and use the air conditioning vents if necessary. Your mileage (miles per gallon) at higher speeds will actually be better since open windows at higher speeds will cause the car to experience drag, meaning it will be less aerodynamically efficient. This "wind throb" was prevented by front window vents on older cars.

Pulling into or out of a Driveway

If you are pulling into or out of a driveway or parking lot, or especially a street where there is a clear cut dip in the curb entrance or exit, or both, go slow and preferably take it at an angle. Often in this situation there is no warning that there is an unusual dip.

Fuel Conservation and Courtesy

If you drive over 60 mph, you will use more gas. Jack rabbit starts and quick sudden stops will use up more gasoline. Also, unnecessary air conditioning will do the same and you should use your vents rather than opening your windows because the windows will cause a drag on the car. If you are trying to slow down and gradually coast to a stop because you see a red light or stop sign up ahead, that is fine, especially if you are alone on the road. But if there is a driver behind you, there may be a courtesy in hitting a happy medium in that regard. That is particularly true if there is a left turn lane up ahead and a the car behind you is trying to get into that left turn lane in order to make the left turn arrow and you are just poking along trying to save gas, holding up the car behind you.

It is better to fill up your car with gas in the early morning or late in the evening because if you fill it up in the middle of the day, especially in hot weather, gas expands and you may be paying more for less. The daytime is considered safer, however.

Recalls

Watch newspapers for recalls. The Sunday *Chicago Tribune* in the Ride Section used to list those and perhaps other parts of the *Chicago Tribune* and other newspapers still do as well. Watch your mail and always open a recall notice, or if you hear it on the radio or television, call your dealer. If you move, be sure to notify the dealer and the company of your new address so that they are able to contact you. Safety recalls are extremely important, particularly when it comes to malfunctions that can cause tire failure, fires, brake or steering failure.

There have been an extreme number of recalls in 2014, 2015 and even into 2016. Actually millions of cars were recalled by General Motors because of a defective ignition switch which would turn off under certain circumstances, even as simple as being bumped by a knee, and this would cause the air bags and the power brakes and power steering to be inoperative, and the car would no longer be powered. Initially there were 13 deaths and more recently there have been more deaths reported and more complaints to be investigated. There have also been extensive recalls on air bags made by Takata, a company in Japan. These airbags could sometimes inadvertently inflate, i.e. with or without any crash or collision, and would sometimes spray shrapnel-like particles toward the driver and the front passenger. Recently this has been reported to even happen with side airbags. Unfortunately, in both of these situations, the repairs were sometimes inadequate or the replacement was also defective and the companies were not able to provide the correct repair or replacement on a timely basis. The regulatory agencies are investigating this troublesome state of affairs. **Log on to safercars.gov/ vin and enter your car's VIN number, and they will notify you of open recalls on your vehicle**. Many Jeeps that had gas tanks to the rear of the rear axle also resulted in tragic fires when these vehicles were struck from behind, and that is another issue that has come to the fore recently. Actually recalls involve all makes of cars and you just simply have to be alert and periodically check with the dealer and check the VIN number with safercar. gov. More recently, Toyota has even recommended that in a car that has not yet been able to be satisfactorily modified after the airbag recall, a passenger should sit in the back seat rather than in the front passenger seat. Since the driver side may also be affected in some instances, it is also recommended that you either lease a car or try to find some other means of transportation until this issue has been resolved. In October 2016, it became apparent that many Volkswagens (those with certain diesel engines, including Audi and Porsche) had cheated on their emission testing and had set up software so that some of their diesel cars would pass emission testing, but once on the road or the highway, they would pollute up to 9 times more than the allowed amount. This affected some 11 million vehicles worldwide. The Volkswagen issue was not necessarily a safety issue for the car occupants, but is an environmental hazard and may decrease the trade-in or resell value of the car, and performance regarding mileage per gallon. There can be important recalls on any car on many days, so be alert. In April 2016, one million GM pick-up trucks were recalled because of defective seatbelts needing repairs.

The Ford Motor Company recalled hundreds of *Windstars* because of an axle problem in late September of 2015. Fiat Chrysler recalled 1.4 million vehicles because it was found out that they could be hacked, which could be dangerous. This had not been reported to have actually occurred yet. Ford recalled many Focus models because door latches were defective.

Some Fiat Chrysler models have had recent reports (February, 2016) of seriously confusing electronic shifting, causing accidents and injuries. Check with safercar.gov, NHTSA.gov or a local dealership.

If you have a problem with your car, and there are three documented failed attempts to fix it, then this qualifies it as a lemon and there is a Lemon Law in many states which enables you to ask for replacement. Sometimes car dealers will ask you to sign a clause which will commit you to arbitration which could lead to repair or replacement. Each state may be different.

Jan Schakowsky, a congresswoman from Illinois, along with several colleagues, has proposed a bill to extend notification of recalls from 10 years after the car was built, up to 20 years, or even to have no time limit. Since a significant percentage of cars affected by recalls are older than 10 years, this makes sense, and I applaud her and her colleague's efforts in that direction.

Turning Left Over Safety Lanes or Islands

If you are turning left over a safety lane or island, if it is legal, try to stay parallel with the safety lane or island so that you don't obstruct traffic from either direction. This is true whether you are turning from a street over a safety island into a parking lot, or you are coming out of a parking lot and turning left and going over a safety lane or island. In this latter situation, you could put yourself parallel onto the safety lane or island, and then when traffic permits, you can enter a lane using your signals. In many areas it is strictly against the law to go over safety lanes or islands, so check out your municipality or state.

Kids Left Alone in Cars

Unfortunately, children left alone in cars, at any age, can do many things that can cause damage or even injury. If the keys are taken out of the car, it is very unlikely that they will be able to start the car. Kids left in cars with keys have been known to start the car and cause horrendous accidents. Even without the keys, a child can sometimes put certain cars into neutral or take off the parking brake or do something else that will cause the car to move into a lane of traffic, if it is on a hill.

The other problem with leaving kids alone in the car is that it is unsafe from the standpoint of criminal activity, and also the child could suffocate in a car or could have a heat related injury or death in the summer. The same is true of cold related injury or death in the winter.

Put the gear in park, turn off the engine, apply the parking brake and take the keys, but remember it is irresponsible to leave young kids alone in a car, and in most situations, it is also illegal.

Traveling with Kids

Make sure you have activities for the kids so that they can handle the boredom that sometimes is present, and that kids are noted for. Be sure that you stop every two hours to rest, and be sure that when you refuel or take pit stops, that kids use the washroom for sure so that they don't have to suddenly have that need ten miles down the road when and where there is no nearby facility.

Road Hazards (Bad Roads or Hazards that may appear suddenly)

There are numerous types of hazards; rocks, mud, and other things falling off or coming down from mountains, or furniture, ladders or merchandise coming off of trucks. Even chemicals can cause hazardous road conditions. Both dirt and gravel roads make stopping or turning more difficult and you are more likely to skid and lose control on a gravel or dirt road. Also be aware that a muddy road could entrap you and you might be stuck even in a 4-wheel drive vehicle. Rock or mud slides that partially or completely block a road may occur in hilly or mountainous regions.

U-Turns

U-turns should usually not be made near intersections and they are illegal in many areas. Often there are signs showing that u-turns are illegal, and there are also signs to show where they are allowed. If you are turning right on red, particularly watch for a car coming from your right making a u-turn right into the same lane that you are turning into. I have seen a sign in a suburb north of Chicago that says "cars making u-turns must yield to cross traffic cars turning 'Right on Red'."

Windshield

All the windows, front windshield, rear and side windows should be kept clean since clear vision is so important for safe driving. There are winter wiper blades which are more likely to be able to clear snow and ice and less likely to stick, and these are available at auto supply stores and many hardware stores. Some car dealers may also be able to install these. Much of windshield vision is covered in the section on winter driving. Products which keep water from obstructing vision on windshields may also be helpful.

Catalogs

The only catalog that I was able to find was Auto Sport and I suspect there may be many more. There are automotive books and magazines in book stores and other stores that one would expect to indicate a number of other automotive catalogs, but even going through several, I did not find automotive catalogs. Auto Sport is *www.autosportcatalog.com* and they have a number of safety items such as emergency folding shovels, electronic roadside emergency beacons, and so-called smart booster cables, supposedly that can't be hooked up wrong. Some of these items are maintenance free lead-acid batteries in a rugged high impact molded case, and some of them, the more expensive ones, also have air inflators (compressors).

This catalog, probably like other similar catalogs, has convex blind spot mirrors that can be attached onto a side view mirror, folding safety triangles, the so-called Original Life Hammer to break a window and/or cut a seat belt, wide angle blind spot rear and side view mirrors, Doze-Alerts, tire gauges, cordless compressors and even tire pressure monitors for cars that don't have the built-in system. They also have Sun Zapper glare shields. A number of interesting items are available at Target stores including reflective safety vests, first aid kits and other auto accessories. Many similar safety oriented items are available at hardware stores including Ace Hardware, and in the Chicago and Midwest area, Menards, and around the country at probably many other hardware and auto parts stores. Amazon.com is another source

Car Thefts

Certain cars, particularly standard sedans that are popular, are the object of thefts more often and one should always lock their car and keep any valuable objects out of sight. It is not unusual for someone to break a car window just to steal a pair of sunglasses.

Equipment to Keep in the Glove Compartment

For the glove compartment you especially need proof of insurance, and if traveling out of state, it is a good idea to have your state registration papers. Also in the glove compartment, keep coins for parking meters (many take credit cards or mobile devices), air pressure gauges for tire checking, extra sunglasses, a small flashlight with extra batteries, other items such as a small first aid kit, a pad of paper and a pen and/or pencil and a disposable camera (if you can find one) if you don't have a cell phone with a camera, or a digital camera that you carry on your person or in your purse. A center console may also be available, but is less likely to have a lock. A bright yellow cloth takes up very little space. A tactical flashlight that has the ability to blink or strobe and zoom is recommended. I would only use regular batteries, having extra ones on hand.

Equipment to Keep in Trunk

For the trunk you need triangles for warning when your car is disabled, railroad fuses, which are harder to use and may only stay lit for a short time. If you are not experienced with them, you're probably better off using triangles. You should have a folding shovel or even a regular small snow shovel for winter conditions. In the winter for a rear wheel drive car, possibly keep a 50 pound bag of sand or kitty litter, and remnants of carpeting or mats in the trunk to help in case you are stuck in snow or ice. The extra weight of the sand is often helpful in snow in a rear wheel drive car, but as mentioned, in a front wheel drive car it may be counter-productive. Also, jumper cables and instructions for using them, or a jump starter, which basically is a charged battery, can be useful. It is a good idea in the wintertime to have extra clothing. If there is a chance of being stuck, or you are taking a longer trip, take water and food supplies as well as extra light sources. A small mirror can be used for signaling help. Also useful to keep in the trunk is duct tape and baling wire, along with a pair of long nose pliers, and other tools.

Airbags

In 2015 and 2016, there were a record number of recalls because of Takata airbags, as mentioned, and these were installed in up to fourteen makes of cars. Originally these recalls were 2001 model and often extending into 2007 and 2008. There has been some indication that this may apply to even more recent cars. This is a potentially major problem, and tens of millions of Takata airbags are out there. It may take years to replace them.

You can go to the government's Takata page which is *www.safercar. gov/rs/takata/ index.html* and enter your vehicles identification number, i.e. your VIN number. You could also just go to safercar.gov and they'll lead you into that or you could also search at Takata airbag recall and you'll eventually get to the same place. By the time you read this book, it is possible that many, if not most, of these recalled vehicles will appear on the website.

> **Remember that recalls are an ongoing process. You can also call your dealer.**

It may take up to two and a half years or longer to make the 33.8 million inflators that are necessary to repair all the cars involved in the Takata recall. The company states that it is making a half a million of these parts per month with plans to produce up to 1 million a month. Some automotive companies may line up other sources to make replacements. This raises a big question, and mostly, but not exclusively, these are driver and passenger side airbags that can inflate with too much force, projecting metal shards out at drivers and passengers, and this may also apply ultimately to side airbags. There have been at least eleven deaths and over 100 injuries worldwide as of the writing of this book. From a practical point of view, besides finding a car that is not involved, and signing up to be on the list to have the airbag replaced in cars with recalls, the other thing that you could do is try even harder to avoid any collision that would cause inflation of your airbag. As I have mentioned before, airbags have deployed without any specific cause, and have even failed to deploy, all of which point out that no system is fail-proof, but this problem is of greater magnitude than has ever been encountered before.

Some Takata replacements have also been shown to be defective and will again have to be replaced. At the time of this book writing, it was felt that explosion was most likely to occur in hot humid climates. Not all of the recalled cars are in the United States. You also may try to get permission from NHTSA to turn off the airbags. Even with authorization you may have difficulty in finding someone to disconnect the airbags, with preferably a switch that can be turned off and on, sometimes with the car key. Some might choose to lease or buy a new or used car, preferably and hopefully without Takata airbags. Toyota has even recommended turning the airbags off until they are replaced. In affected cars, front passengers are advised to sit in the back seat, prior to proper airbag replacement. Some other companies that manufacture airbags have also been implicated in defective products, and the recall may eventually extend into cars manufactured into the middle teens of the 21st century. The older an airbag is, the more likely it will explode on deployment. Recently o-rings that have been degreased have been found to allow moisture to enter the beads which then clump together and may cause the explosion.

Takata agreed to stop using nondesiccated ammonium nitrate as the inflator in future airbags (by 2018) but would continue using desiccated ammonium nitrate. Other airbag manufacturers are switching from ammonium nitrate, but dates and details are not available as of this writing. The reports have been conflicting, and the situation is fluid.

Insurance

It is very important to insure with a reliable insurance company. I have long been insured with State Farm Insurance, and I do receive a discount for a safe, accident and traffic ticket free driving record. Up until November 16, 2016 they had a program which connects a small device into the onboard diagnostic port (OBD-11), the same port mechanics use for diagnostic scanning. Driving at legal speed, lower accident rate time of day, and with no jack-rabbit starts, sudden or hard braking, or long distances, lead to modest reduction of auto insurance premiums. That program, with reasonable cost, also provided a visor mounted GPS, which could connect to emergency medical help, automotive assistance, and Bluetooth, They now recommend Hum.com, by Verizon. This does not necessarily lead to an insurance premium reduction. It does provide GPS, Bluetooth, direct contact for medical, mechanical, emergency accident help, as well as diagnostics, and alerts for restricted driving limits for teenagers, connected to a parent's smartphone. I recommend interested drivers or parents check this website or contact their insurance company. OnStar is available for most GM cars, and this can provide a number of emergency and safety functions, including notification of airbag deployment. T- mobile users can check-out T-MobileSyncUPDRIVE, as of December 13,2016. This can be connected to your Smartphone. I would again recommend interested drivers check this website or contact their insurance company. OnStar is available for most GM cars and this also provides a number of automatic safety functions including emergency notification when an airbag has deployed. There may be additional costs for these safety features, including stolen car location and shut down with OnStar. With Hum.com, you can also set an area that your teenager can not go beyond, and also a speed limit for them as well.

The Automatic™ App and Automatic Pro also plugs into the OBD-11 port in most cars sold since 1996. This connects to the Internet by means of a Smartphone, and offers important basic features without ongoing monthly costs. Five years of service are included. You don't have to recharge it, since it draws power from your car. A serious accident triggers a crash alert cellular connection. An agent will call you, and if you don't respond, will communicate with emergency services. The agent will then call your listed emergency contact. Except in areas without cellular service, this works even if your cell phone is turned off or broken. The Automatic and Automatic Pro doesn't help in non-emergency situations. It will also help in locating a stolen car. Although the Automatic has some advantages, if you had an incapacitating medical emergency without a crash, it would not be as helpful as Hum (by Verizon) or some other devices. It could help you find your car in a crowded parking lot. The Automatic Pro is the second generation. I have no personal experience with this adapter.

How to Jump Start a Car with a Dead Battery

First of all, pull the car with the live battery up near the car with the dead battery, but not touching. In the car with the dead battery, turn off all switches, heating, air conditioning, radio and everything else, including lights. Put the car in park and put the parking brake on. Safety glasses are strongly recommended. After opening the car's hoods, attach the red positive (+) clamp of one cable to the positive battery post of the dead car. Next attach the red positive (+) clamp to the positive post of the live car. Next, attach the black negative (-) clamp to the negative battery post of the live car. Then attach the black negative (-) clamp onto an area close to the engine but not on the actual battery post. If using the sheet metal of the car, use an unpainted portion. The reason for not putting the black negative clamp onto the actual battery post is because that could cause an explosion. Next run the engine of the live car for three minutes slightly above idling, approximately 2,000 rpm if you have a tachometer. Next, try to start the dead car. If the dead car doesn't start, turn the engine off and run the live car for five to ten minutes and try again. Sometimes moving the clamps to a different position, particularly on the dead car, will be helpful. If the dead car then starts, undo the jumper cables in the reverse order they were applied, i.e. first remove the negative clamp from the car that was dead, then from the live car, and then remove the positive clamp from the live car, and finally the positive clamp from the previously dead car. Avoid touching the clamps together and also make sure the cars are not touching each other. The dead car that has been started should be run at slightly higher than idle to charge the battery for at least five to ten minutes. It can then be driven but the motor should not be shut off for at least 20 minutes, to allow the batter to continue to charge. Ordinarily it would be driven to a service station or to home or another place where, should it not restart, it will not be in an unsafe spot, and there will be another car or cars to jump it again if needed. Use a heavy gauge jumper cable. (The lower the number, the heavier the gauge.)

WINTER SAFETY HINTS FOR PEDESTRIANS

I'D ALSO LIKE TO OFFER SAFETY hints for pedestrians during the winter, especially in areas where there is ice and snow. Drivers become pedestrians and wet surfaces could be tricky anytime of the year:

- Have deep tread on your shoes, or wear overshoes or boots. Avoid worn-smooth leather soles. Choose anti-slip extra traction soles, when available.
- Hold onto railings.
- Take small (baby) steps.
- Keep a container of "ice melting salt" for winter use in the house and in the car. Spread it before each few steps on ice. If you are getting out of the car onto a parking lot or street where there is ice, particularly black ice, put a little salt where you step out of your car. That will increase your traction. Keep the salt with you if necessary to sprinkle it ahead of you in a really icy situation.
- A Wilmette police officer, Daniel Huck, has pointed out to me that since the police carry heavy equipment, drivers are taught to turn to the left as they exit the car and to put both feet down at the same time, so as not to put unusual stress on one leg or the other. This is good advice and probably will also decrease the number of slippages or falls when getting out of your car, especially on a slippery surface.
- When exiting a car, hold onto the door handle or a stable part of the car while planting preferably both feet onto the surface to be certain it is not slippery.

ADDITIONAL REMINDERS

Cruise Control – Do not use cruise control if you are drowsy, or if there is rain, snow or ice.

Carrying Gasoline – Never carry gasoline inside the car – It should only be in the gas tank.

Weather Alerts – AAA has an app for weather alerts and they can send these out to five different locations for members, relatives or friends.

Panic Buttons – If you are using the panic button on your car to try to make noise and attract attention, if you suspect, with cars parked outside, that there may be some tampering or other disturbance, make sure the batteries are fresh and check it out from different floors of your house. In an apartment building it may not work, depending upon the location and/ or distance to your car.

Autonomous or Semi-Autonomous Cars – Many domestic (including Tesla) and foreign car manufacturers are developing semi-autonomous or autonomous cars. Google and Apple are cooperating with car manufacturers in this regard. Google has a number of cars on certain California highways that have racked up significant miles. There have been accidents which are claimed to be the result of a non-autonomous car, but the verdict is still out. These cars use a variety of radar, lasers and cameras tied into computers to sense obstructions and eventually even pedestrians and bicyclists hopefully, and to enable them to safely turn left against opposing traffic. Volvo's XC-90 already has enough automation to make it semi-autonomous. These vehicles still require that a driver be seated and be able to take over quickly if necessary, at least for the present.

There are also some lines of semi-autonomous trucks which also require a driver, but do take some of the strain and fatigue off of the driver for highway driving. Also software has been available for several years for combines and other farm equipment as well as industrial equipment, which can pretty much operate autonomously. My take at this point, in mid-2016, is that the prediction of 2019 or 2020 may be a little premature and there are many legal and technical difficulties to be worked out before one could probably feel reasonably safe in this situation. It may be a step-wise progression. I'm again reminded of the loud speaker on a commercial airliner announcing to the passengers; *"Sit back and relax, this is an all computerized plane, and there is no pilot. Nothing can go wrong, go wrong, go wrong, go wrong, go wrong."* (I am not the originator of this potentially relevant humor.)

I do think autonomous cars are in our future and my guess is 2025, but it is only a guess. Recognizing other vehicles, and being able to connect with them may be one of the important parts of the development of this coming era, as well as operating in severe weather conditions. I think they will have to make sure that these autonomous cars can read signs, including small signs that say "Left Turn On Arrow Only," and they can read traffic lights, including making decisions when traffic lights are malfunctioning and/or when road signs are unreadable because of blizzard or other conditions. They'll also have to be able to tell construction zones, no turns, and other similar warning devices and signs. Eventually they may be able to work this out, but I think it will be much longer then presently predicted, so there will need to be somebody in the driver's seat, and if it were me, I would want a steering wheel and pedals and a means to be able to immediately take control.

The more complex cars become with newer safety and other advanced features, the more opportunity for confusion, and even malfunction and the need for service. Be certain you understand all the features of any car you drive, and how to handle them without distraction.

Speed Monitoring – In Chicago, there is photographic monitoring of speed on roads adjacent to or near public and private schools, and also park districts. Usually with the first offense you will get a letter indicating the time, the date, the street and your speed and how to access a photo on the Internet. This will be a warning and the next time a ticket will accompany that.

Run Off the Road – If you run off the road, either accidentally or if you are run off the road, many experts advise just gradually getting back on. They caution against turning the wheel too sharply since it might have adverse effects. My experience with over six decades of driving is that if there is a grade separation between the shoulder and the road, and you try to get on gradually, sometimes that will be trickier then cutting it rather sharply. I would hope that most beginning drivers find a place with their instructor that they can practice this technique. Of course you need to make sure that when you are re-entering the road, it is safe to do so.

Left Turns – When waiting in the intersection for a light to change for a left turn, try to monitor the stop light as well, and as soon as you see that has turned to caution or red, then check to make sure that cars are stopping or have stopped before proceeding to make the left turn. This way, you won't be stuck in the middle of the intersection and you won't hold up an additional car (or two) that might be in the intersection behind you also waiting to complete their turn. If there is any question that an opposing or cross traffic car is not stopping, then be patient and wait.

Seat Cushions – Seat cushions may inactivate the airbag on the drivers' side. Drivers who use seat cushions on the driver's seat should check to see if it is necessary to remove the seat cushion. Heavy items placed on the passenger's seat may simulate a passenger's weight and activate the airbag in case of a crash.

Parking Lot Vision Adjustment – When going from a well lit building to a dark parking lot, stay just inside or just outside the door for several minutes to let your eyes accommodate (adjust) to the darkness, so that you will be able to more safely access your car.

Pedestrians – Pedestrians, whether walking on the sidewalk or on parkways or on curbs, need to be aware that a driver may lose control of a car which could come up on a sidewalk or any other area. Reasons for this can be mechanical failure, drivers may be "under the influence," or be experiencing a medical problem, or the car may have been involved in an accident, and possibly other causes, including intentional. I've seen the results of this actually happening. Fortunately, there were no persons walking on the sidewalk. The car came from the other side of the street and caused incredible physical damage to the buildings on that side. By being alert you have a better chance of avoiding serious or even fatal injury. Pedestrians should be focused on their surroundings, and not reading, talking, and particularly texting or talking on cell phones, and should be aware that a car can come from any direction and end up where it is not supposed to be, and you as a pedestrian may also be where you are not supposed to be. This has happened in the past; pedestrians in normally protected areas have been seriously and even fatally injured by errant cars due to D.U.I. (Driving Under the Influence), medical emergencies, accidents, and rarely intentional, or other causes. Daily I find pedestrians walking out in front of me, not necessarily in crosswalks, but anywhere, and without even looking up, and often they are not even on a phone. I have seen people carrying babies, pushing strollers, walking dogs, and it is incumbent upon drivers to be aware that pedestrians may not look or may not care if a car is coming and the burden falls upon the driver to be very alert. This is also meant to be a reminder to pedestrians to look and not assume that a car is not coming, or if one is coming, that it is going to stop. This is Basic Survival 101. To some extent the same advice goes to bicyclists and also drivers who have to watch out for bicyclists.

Takata – The Takata airbag recall broke all records for recalls and involves nearly 70 million airbags in approximately 25 million cars, by fourteen automakers, leaving still millions of other Takata airbags that haven't been recalled. It is estimated that one in every five of the 250 million vehicles currently (2016) on U.S. roads could be part of the Takata recall. Takata is supposed to recall even all desiccated ammonium nitrate inflators "by the end of 2019 unless regulators are satisfied that they are safe. The picture is confusing and troubling.

The reason for the ongoing duplication of this matter with Takata airbags is the change from day-to-day and week-to-week of the status of this problem. Reference: *U.S. Doubles Size of Takata Air-Bag* Recall by Mike Spector, The Wall Street Journal. May 5, 2016. BloombergBusinessweek, had, in early June of 2016, a resume of the complex sequence of events at Takata. My suggestion of options is: have the recall taken care of, and retain the documentation; If the dealer has stated that it was already done, or doesn't need to be done, retain that documentation; If you can't get a safe working replacement, possibly lease a car without Takata airbags; Ask front seat passengers in cars that may be at risk, to sit in the back seat. Those back seat airbags may also be defective, especially if made by Takata; Drive carefully, especially with attention to the interval behind the car in front; In some instances, you might choose to have the airbags deactivated, and for that, you may have to obtain permission from NHTSA, and find a mechanic equipped to deactivate the airbags. Airbags do save lives, and you are somewhat caught between a rock and a hard place. These dangerous explosions are more likely to occur in older cars and in hot humid climates, especially with wide fluctuations. Some priority is extended to replacement in those areas. Takata plans to continue to supply airbags with ammonium nitrate without a desiccant, i.e. a drying agent, into 2018 or 2019, and this could be a continuing problem. I would advise drivers buying or leasing cars to be certain that their airbags are not made by Takata and do not contain ammonium nitrate. Guanidine nitrate is a substitute that appears at this time to be safe. Hopefully, this situation will be corrected. Be certain that the driver's airbag is pointed toward the chest, and not the neck, face, or head.

Check Your Car's Manual – Check your car's manual for the presence of and the significance of different icons on the instrument panel indicating safety features and indications of problems. Be certain that you understand these

Gear Shifting – In late June 2016 there was an extensive recall of Jeep Grand Cherokees due to confusion regarding gear shifting. Apparently the car would end up in neutral and would roll in a number of instances. Jeep Grand Cherokee owners should make sure they are contacting their dealership.

Buds in the Ears – Drivers are requested not to ever use buds in both ears. Some courses teach that you can have one bud in one ear, but only after the age of 19. Check your local ordinances in regard to that. It is far better to not be distracted while driving, and also to be able to hear as well as possible.

Recalls – Recalls appear almost daily so that no book or article can be up-to-date. Drivers are encouraged to check sources, particularly the National Highway Traffic Safety Administration (NHTSA) website, which is safercar.gov. You can also ask to be put on a list to be automatically notified of a recall for the car that you own, giving them either the VIN number or the license plate.

On June 30, 2016, an Internet posting stated that Honda had asked for assistance from the media and the public to alert owners of three million Hondas and Acuras that their airbags may rupture and cause injury or death. They were actually advised not to drive these cars which were basically 2001 to 2003 or later, and to contact their dealers. At the same time, Acura notified me of a recall on the passenger side airbag in our 2005 MDX. These were Takata airbags. I did not see this mentioned in any other media, but I may have missed it. Practically the same day, Toyota recalled 1.4 million vehicles globally because of defective side curtain airbags deploying in parked and unoccupied vehicles. 495,000 of the recalled vehicles were in North America. These airbags were not made by Takata. Lexus was included in this recall, and there was also mention of defective emission control. Around the same time, there was discussion in the media regarding a Tesla Model S car with so-called autopilot which had crashed into an 18 wheeler semi-trailer that had turned in front of it in Florida on May 7, 2016. The trailer was painted white, and the thinking was that it was detected as an overhead sign, since it was a few feet off the ground. Obviously much more work needs to be done to work out these imperfections. The driver of the Tesla, who was killed, reportedly may have been watching a video. This was the first death recorded in a Tesla. It has been reported that Tesla warns buyers that they still need to be paying attention, since the technical mechanics may not be perfect. Unfortunately, Murphy's Law seems to hold, i.e. "whatever can go wrong, will," and again it reverts back to the fact that a majority of accidents are due to driver error, and in this case it may be not following the recommendations of the producer of the equipment. The company had cautioned those who had received the upgrade on the software to still maintain vigilance and control on the road, since to some extent it was not yet perfected. Drivers have been known to be reading newspapers or books or magazines while the car is being trusted to function safely. This pretty much substantiates what I have felt about autonomous and semi-autonomous cars, that they are not yet ready to be safely used, but it is an evolving situation, both from the technical standpoint, and from the governmental regulatory standpoint. Tesla may change the term "autopilot" to a more emphasized cautionary designation.

Mitsubishi was cited for manipulating fuel economy on their cars and the reference for that is the Wall Street Journal, June 18-19, 2016, p. B4. On October 12, 2016, It was reported that there had been over 400 complaints of 2014 an d 2015 Jeep Cherokees stalling while being driven. The problem was felt to be related to the nine speed automatic transmission.

Student Drivers – When a student driver is taking a lesson, it is a good idea to have some kind of identification on the car. This could be something on the top of the car, or it could be a magnetic sign saying, "Student Driver, thank you for your patience," or it could be simply a bumper sticker with adhesive, saying something similarly appropriate.

Airplanes – If an airplane seems to be "buzzing" the road that you are on, i.e. flying unusually low over it repeatedly, it is probably the pilot asking you to cooperate and provide a stretch that they can land on. How you react may depend on many circumstances including the width of the highway, how successful you will be in getting other cars coming in that direction, or the other direction, to also cooperate, but you should at least understand what the intention of the buzzing is likely indicating, and contact 9-1-1.

Cell Phone Programming – With your cell phone programmed into your car, or even just by itself, don't program "Call the House," but use a nearby address such as a store. You can also do that in reference to referring to the GPS.

Stopping in Traffic – Stop far enough behind the car in front of you, so that you could pull around it if necessary.

If your check engine light comes on, be sure your gas cap is on tight.

PET PEEVES

(Not necessarily in the order of significance)

My personal pet peeves are:

- Cars driving slowly in the left lane, everybody's pet peeve
- Drivers using cell phones, especially texting, much more prevalent in spite of laws, and very disturbing
- Drivers who are unfocused and are being distracted by anything inside or outside of their car
- Cars that don't stop at stop signs or traffic lights close to the center line or the left lane line, thus not allowing drivers to turn right on red (sometimes just pulling over a foot or two to the left, or pulling forward a foot or two will allow a car on the right to safely get by)
- Drivers that fail to turn on their headlights when the windshield wipers are on, or when visibility is poor
- Horns blaring by the car or truck behind me, and I can't move until the car in front of me moves, this could startle somebody into making a move causing an accident.
- Bicyclists disobeying rules of the road, especially causing unnecessary danger to themselves and/or interference with traffic, often having no lights, and wearing dark clothing, especially at night
- Bicyclists illegally riding two abreast, making passing more difficult
- Tailgating at any speed
- Drivers (and/or passengers) exiting on the driver's side without checking for traffic coming upon them or even coming from the opposite direction

- Driving under the influence of alcohol, drugs including marijuana, and medications (over-the-counter or prescription)
- Drowsy drivers, especially truckers driving large trucks and exceeding the permitted hours in terms of getting rest, and therefore at risk of not being alert
- Going too fast for conditions in parking lots, especially not using headlights and not going slowly past cars that may be backing up, and themselves not backing up slowly until they have a good view of what's coming behind them
- So-called "entitled drivers" who drive up to the front of merging lanes rather then demonstrating a sense of fairness by attempting to merge further back (I disagree with some traffic engineers who advise pulling up to the merge point, expecting drivers who have been waiting, to alternate with them).
- Cars on entrance ramps that use the shoulder to pass cars in front of them that are merging
- Drivers who don't signal turns or lane changes
- Drivers stopping so far behind the car in front that they block exits or entrances
- Cars in left turn lanes that don't pull up far enough to trigger the left turn lane signal
- Sewer covers protruding (on recently repaved streets), that have not yet had the tapering around the circumference, and therefore protrude 1/2 inch to an inch above the surface of the road

I'm sure that the readers of *Sane Driving in a Mad World* will have their own list of personal pet peeves. **Remember, nothing justifies getting involved in a road rage incident.**

ACKNOWLEDGMENTS

I AM INDEBTED TO THE ILLINOIS SECRETARY of State, Jesse White, and his staff. I wish to thank the long serving former Wilmette Chief of Police George Carpenter, and Brian King, Chief of Police of the Village of Wilmette for their encouragement on this project. I also appreciate Chief King clarifying certain important questions that I had.

This book also recognizes the contribution of Ralph Nader as one of the early advocates for automotive safety, particularly starting with his book *"Unsafe At Any Speed"* in the early 1960's.

I appreciate the expertise and honesty of Borhan Khatib and Chuck Postma, both of Petersen Automotive in Skokie, IL for their answers to several special technical questions. I would also like to thank all of the members of my family, my friends, colleagues, and former patients who have shown interest and encouragement in regards to this endeavor.

A good friend, Burton Siegal, made me aware of *fixation* as it applies to driving and the importance of understanding the natural tendency to steer the car in the potentially dangerous direction that one is looking. That's an important concept in crash avoidance, especially head-on crash avoidance, where you should be looking at your escape route. Most experienced drivers will learn to adjust and compensate for the tendency of *fixation*.

Without the assistance, patience, expertise and organizational ability of Stephanie Bockhol, at A OK Business Service in Chicago, Illinois I would never have been able to stay organized enough to complete this work.

Robert W. Boxer, M.D.

BOOK SUMMARY: Driving is obviously a complex act, requiring not only concentration but also judgment and experience. I have chosen many important points, but strongly recommend reading the entire book.

- It is important to pick a safe car. The mirrors should be adjusted so that the driver can easily be aware of what's behind, on either side, as well as in front.
- Speeding is a main cause of crashes. The interval between cars is another major factor, and tailgating at high speeds is seen much too often, even at moderate or low speeds.
- Alcohol, other drugs including marijuana, prescription and nonprescription medications, as well as drowsiness can seriously affect driving.
- A well maintained car, with special emphasis on brakes and steering, as well as all lights working, is important.
- There are many distractions inside the car, especially cell phones and texting, which must be avoided, and many distractions outside of the car which should also be avoided. Even hands-free cellphone use is felt to be very distractive.
- Seatbelts and airbags should be utilized and one should be aware of recalls, particularly on airbags, brakes, and other safety issues.
- Use care when entering and exiting your car and be careful not to knock a passing bicyclist or motorcyclist into another lane (which can easily be fatal), or to cause a car to swerve.
- Understand traffic lights in detail, and also that with certain weather conditions they may be difficult to visualize.
- Be cautious and courteous with right turns on red after coming to a complete stop. Always give the right of way to pedestrians.

- At intersections, cover the brake particularly on residential streets, often even ones protected by stop signs and/or traffic lights.
- On narrow residential streets, with an oncoming car, pull into an open space to allow the oncoming car to pass.
- Stay in your lane while driving on expressways and change lanes only after very carefully ascertaining an opening, and signaling.
- When passing another car, and especially a truck, do it rather quickly (don't linger in their blind spot).
- Be aware that trucks take longer to stop, and they often have to make wide turns.
- Watch for obstructions in the road, including things falling off of trucks, or tires or even an entire wheel with its tire, coming off of cars or trucks, and potholes.
- Watch for objects, such as a ball thrown into the road, followed by a child or pet.
- Be especially careful at railroad crossings, and never cross railroad tracks unless there is easily sufficient space on the other side for your car or vehicle. Never go around gates which are down.
- If you see or hear an emergency vehicle, pull over to the right as far as you can and stop, and if you can't pull to the right, at least stop where you are. Be aware that emergency vehicles can be coming from several directions and they may need to turn in front of you, if coming from the opposite direction, and may even need to go on your side of the road.
- Be aware of other drivers, and the signs of bad drivers, i.e. drifting out of their lane, stopping for no reason at all, starting up too slowly when the light changes (If you are the lead car, hesitating for a second or two is encouraged to check for red light runners and emergency vehicles).
- Park in safe places, well lit and close to building entrances.
- Use your lights in parking lots, particularly closed parking garages. Hold onto the car door when you open it, so that it doesn't hit the car next to you. When backing up, go very slowly, a few inches at first, and then still with short distances, until you have good vision and you are aware of a clear path.

- Be aware of the hazards of left turns and the difficulty in judging the speed or even the presence of an oncoming car in any lane, including the opposing curb lane.
- Slow down for speed bumps.
- Don't swerve if a deer comes into your path. Honk your horn and flash your lights, and try to stop.
- Obey reduced speed limits in construction zones, even if there is no construction going on.
- **Do not use cruise control in rain, snow or ice, or if drowsy.**
- Use low beam headlights in a fog.
- Be aware that downed wires can cause a fire, and if you exit the car into water where a downed live wire is in contact, you'll likely be electrocuted. Even dry ground can be electrified up to 35 feet away from a downed live wire. See page 64.
- Be aware of how difficult sunshine delay can be, not only in the morning and early evening, but also at any time during the day, coming off of your car, another car, even buildings.
- With winter driving, with snow and/or ice, try not to turn and accelerate or brake at the same time. Drive according to conditions at all times, which means that you could be going very slowly in severe weather and road conditions.
- Avoid road rage, either inciting it or responding to incitement from another driver.
- Use your brakes instead of your horn, although use the horn if necessary to avoid a crash.
- Be aware of the graduated licensing laws and the application of these to beginning drivers, particularly the number of passengers carried as well as the hours of practice needed to fulfill the requirements for licensing.
- If senior drivers are having difficulty with vision or cognition or reflexes, they may benefit by contacting the occupational therapy department of their local hospital.
- Understand the meaning of all roadway signs and obey them.
- Be responsible for your passengers and don't even move the car until all occupants of the car have buckled their seatbelt. Alert

them to the safest way to exit the car, both for their safety and for the safety of passing cars, trucks, motorcycles, and bicycles.

- Use courtesy at all times, except when it may endanger the driver to whom you are extending it.
- Check tires at least monthly and be aware that tires over six years old may need to be replaced, or at least checked. If you can see the head of President Lincoln when a penny is inserted into the tread, it is time to replace the tire.
- Understand how to respond to a flat tire or blow out (page 106).
- Don't get back into the car when refueling with gasoline. Even when first getting out, touch the front car door or the station's metal bars to discharge your static electricity before going to the gas tank and the gas pump.
- Share the road with motorcyclists, who have the right to a complete lane.
- Share the road with bicyclists and give them at least three feet of clearance when passing them.
- Stop for school buses according to their flashing lights and stop sign, and wait until they have left the area before passing to avoid hitting children who may be crossing in front of or behind the bus.
- When renting a car, or using a loaner, pick one that you are familiar with, or make sure that you familiarize yourself with all the important functions of the car before leaving the lot.
- If you end up in water, try to open your windows immediately while they may still work. Unbuckle your seatbelt. If the water is deep, you may be able to leave the vehicle through the window, door or sun roof. If the water is not that deep, you may choose to stay with the car until you are rescued, but be aware that if the water is moving you downstream, there may be deadly hazards ahead. Unlock the doors and turn the headlights on. Read the section in this book on water entrapment (page 106).
- Avoid hydroplaning with wet roads by controlling your speed. If you do hydroplane, take your foot off the accelerator until you have regained traction.
- Be aware of the danger of avalanches and rock slides in mountainous areas.

- High winds can buffet the car sufficiently to put it into another lane, so have two hands on the wheel at all times, and drive only if necessary if there are unusually strong winds.
- With earthquakes, try to get away from tall buildings or trees, but avoid going under or over bridges or overpasses which could collapse onto or under your car.
- Don't cross or drive on a road if there is water on it, especially if it is up to the exhaust pipe of other cars in front of you.
- Try to pull into a shelter if there is a hail storm.
- Don't stay in your car if you are caught in a tornado. Get out and seek the lowest possible spot, preferably a ditch or culvert. Lie down and cover your head with your hands.
- Be aware that rollovers of large trucks can be dangerous for everybody in the vicinity. Do not cut off any cars or trucks.
- With a stuck gas pedal, put the car in neutral and pull off the road. If it is a manual transmission, put the clutch in and then put the gear in neutral.
- If you are involved in an accident, you need to exchange information and tend to injured persons, as well as to notify authorities. If you encounter an accident on the road or off to the side of the road, follow the advice given in this book (pages 117-118).
- Traffic stops by police officers require that you produce your license and your insurance documentation. Turn your dome light on if it is at night. Keep your hands where the officer can see them, make the officer feel comfortable and safe. Do not argue, if there is reason to contest the stop, do that in court. Mention any extenuating circumstances before a ticket is written. Stay in your car unless requested otherwise by the police officer.
- Be aware that carjacking can occur anywhere, including your garage, your driveway, where you are parked, or even at a filling station or at a restaurant parking lot. It may even occur in slow moving traffic.
- Don't interfere with or interrupt a funeral procession. Be respectful and patient
- Use updated GPS units intelligently, ask a passenger to enter change of destination or do this while stopped.

- Give explicit directions to other drivers using points of reference such as landmarks and distances.
- When driving in the mountains, be particularly aware of black ice on the shady side of the mountain, and/or black ice even on level roads.
- Always respond to recalls.
- **Review this entire book because it is difficult to summarize all the many points included.**
- Always signal at least 100 feet ahead of a turn, unless there is a street, alley, or parking lot exit before you turn. Remember to turn off your signals after pulling out of a parking space, changing lanes, or making a half turn into or from an angle street.
- Do not leave small children, pets or the elderly alone in a car for many reasons, including in the winter when they can freeze, or in the summer when they can suffocate or suffer heat stroke.
- If traveling in the winter, have sufficient supplies in the car in case you become stuck, particularly in a blizzard. Review that part of *"Sane Driving in a Mad World"*.
- Ideally have a spare tire and make sure tire inflation is checked at least monthly, and the spare tire at least yearly. Alternatively, have a non-flammable pressurized sealer and an inflator, or all of the above.
- Do not sit too close to airbags, be at least 10 inches, preferably 12 inches away, and have the driver's side airbag pointed at your chest rather than your neck, face, and head.
- Have infant and child car seats checked by specialists.
- When entering your car, do a walk-around, noticing low tires, and any evidence of tampering.
- Read your state's Rules of the Road, ideally every year.
- Read your car's drivers manual and keep it in the car.
- Be especially careful when turning left at busy intersections. Be aware that when your light changes to yellow or red, the light for oncoming traffic may still be green.
- Be courteous to other drivers who may need to change lanes or to enter an expressway.

- Understand that Merge means reaching the speed of cars in the right lane and entering that lane if there is an opening, using your turn signals. Yield means stop if necessary.
- Always give pedestrians the right of way. Pedestrians should stay focused, follow the law, make eye contact with drivers, and also show courtesy.
- Turn your headlights on if the weather or visibility is poor, and use your headlights whenever windshield wipers, even your interval wipers, are on.
- Follow the "Golden Rule" and treat others (drivers, pedestrians, bicyclists, motorcyclists, emergency responders, construction workers, and police officers), as you would like to be treated if the circumstances were reversed.

RESOURCES, INCLUDING WEBSITES

(Only the title may be indicated, which is often the only part necessary to bring up the website.)

- **Safercars.gov.** The website of safercar.gov provides information relative to recalls and also a considerable amount of other driving safety material.
- **National Highway Traffic Safety Administration (NHTSA).** This website includes recalls and filing of complaints as well a considerable amount of other useful information.
- **Insurance Institute for Highway Safety (IIHS).** This institute is funded by the auto insurance companies. It is especially useful for safety testing of cars..
- **American Automobile Association (AAA also called Triple A)** and their Foundation. The AAA provides roadside service for which it is probably best known for, useful Triptix, travel planning and maps, auto and accident insurance, also hotel and auto rental discounts. Their publications (AAA Living sent to members), have considerable information on safety aspects. They also are good for contracts between parents and teenage drivers. They offer free membership to teen aged drivers, who are children of parents with membership in AAA. They also offer other benefits. I have been a member for at least three decades, if not longer, and have been very satisfied with their services. AAA Living May/June 2016 – Roadwise RX, is apparently a website tool to see how your medication would be impacting your driving ability. They also suggest having a driver planning agreement which means in part

to have a guide to help families explore application options for continued safe mobility, and this is referring to older drivers.

- **www.aaa.com/asc-new-roadwisereview.asp.** This is a website where you can check visual, physical, and mental abilities. Go to www.aaasouth.com/acs_news/ roadwisereview to order an online self-assessment for $15.00.

- **AAA.com/weather.** Free for AAA members. A weather alert for dangerous weather, it can be automatically sent to five different locations.

- **AAAdrivers55+,** this website provides a self-rating online quiz. It leads into other websites including 65+ and others by AAA.

- **AAAfoundation.org,** this is the website for the AAA Foundation for traffic safety which is for teen drivers as well as seniors. You can purchase ($29.95) an interactive video to help make you a Driver ZED (Zero Error Driver). This is a two hour interactive risk management training video. Interestingly, they mention that falls in adults are associated with an increased risk of motor vehicle accidents. I hope that this will be further researched.

- **Teendriving.aaa.com** or **Keys2drive** A Guide to Teen Driving Safety, this is a website that educates parents on safety and it is a resource for parents and teens for the learning-to-drive experience. According to AAA "distracted driving amongst teens is a much greater problem than previously thought, with passengers and cell phones being the most common causes of distraction." This leads you to Parent/Teen driving agreement and also free online teen driver safety resources and student driver and traffic safety educational materials.

- **SafeSeats4Kids**. This is another Triple A website, very useful for finding a child car seat inspection station near you, and much more.

- **AOL Autos.** This website often has relevant safety as well as other useful information.

- **Kelley Blue Book (KBB.com).** This is a useful resource for determining the price of used cars and new cars as well. They publish a hard copy guide. This is a subsidiary of AutoTrader.com, Inc. They list market value prices for new and used vehicles, also expert consumer reviews and "Five Year Cost to Own" on new cars which I suspect has to be an estimate, and also they offer online auto shopping.

- **Motoring News.** They provide expert opinion on various aspects of cars including safety. They do have a car price quote service and other pricing information.

- **Edmunds.** This website provides car tips and advice, also new and used car reviews, and prices. Edmunds.com has "Price Promise," and also selling tips and car research. They have what's called the Black Book (versus Kelley Blue Book). The Black Book seems more for valuations for dealers and lenders and less for drivers in general. This is, in my opinion, often a very useful website. Cars.com also has a black book and I don't know how that interfaces with the one by Edmunds. You can get the specific information by going to the general website such as cars.com or Edmunds.com or kelleybluebook.com.

- **Cars.com.** They have access to service estimates and advice, as well as recalls and car maintenance and review. They also assist in buying, selling and trading cars. **If you are checking to see if you have had a reasonable price estimate on a repair, this is one resource that you might use.** Their car reviews often appear in the *Chicago Tribune*.

- **Mothers Against Drunk Driving (MADD).** This website has information on drunk and drugged driving, support for victims, and is also involved in the prevention of underage drinking.

- **Students Against Destructive Decisions** (Formerly Students Against Drunk Driving, SADD, but the scope has evolved and widened). This organization is involved in tools to help prevent drunk and drugged driving, and other destructive decisions by students, which includes indulging in not only drinking, and drugs, but also risky and impaired driving.

- **American Association of Retired Persons (AARP).** They produce pamphlets and booklets which include information of interest to people who are members (who are over 50) but also frequently have information on driving safety and other concerns regarding driving in an older population. They do offer a variety of consumer products including insurance. AARP also prominently offers driving safety advice and courses in driving safety for mature adults, as well as many other services. www.aarp.org/family/ driversafetyissues, has driver safety courses which you can probably access just by going to AARP.org.

- **AARP.org**/families/driver_safety/driver_safetyissues/a_2014-26whentostop.html. This website pretty much goes over the same questions as the AAA risk assessment quiz.
- **Consumer Reports.org.** This monthly magazine and occasional special issue is very useful from the standpoint of purchasing both new and used automobiles, their reliability, their safety testing as well as general reviews of new cars and the comparison of cars. They list cars according to value, even looking at the cost of operating it over a number of years, and they do offer a buying service and guide. I have been a subscriber for the last 30 or 40 years and have found it consistently valuable for a number of items, prominently including cars
- **National Safety Council**, sometimes called NSC. They have an emphasis on driving safety, particularly defensive driving courses, and *Safety On The Road*. It is a good website to look into. They've apparently shown that the brain activity that processes moving images decreases by up to 1/3 when listening to/or talking on a phone. They also have interesting statistics on alcohol, speeding, and distracted driving in relation to fatalities.
- *Chicago Tribune.* They have transportation news including major car recalls in the main section of the paper. They have a Sunday section called *Rides* which has occasional features by Jim Mateja, and also a regular column by Bob Weber dealing with all kinds of automotive problems, including maintenance as well as safety. I've been reading this regularly for many years and find it quite useful. They have car reviews by cars.com and by others.
- **Blue Cross/Blue Shield of Illinois publications**. They have information on driving safety, besides health, life style and insurance.
- **Wall Street Journal**. They have good coverage of vehicle news including recalls and they cover the economic, political and legal

impact of some of the major defects that have turned up in cars. They have car reviews by Dan Neil, of The Los Angeles Times

- **Carfax** is a resource when buying or selling a car. They have much information regarding the past history of the cars they are selling or buying. It is still a good idea to take any car that you are thinking of purchasing to a trusted mechanic to have them look it over very carefully, and to make sure it hasn't been involved in a flood.

- **AutoCheck.** This is another service somewhat similar to CarFax but they don't sell cars. They have a full report regarding whether the car has been reported to have been in an accident, branded a 'lemon' or a total loss, such as damaged in a flood, or reported repossessed or stolen, and more.

- **Tradeinexpert.com.** This is a subsidiary of Cars.com. This gives trade-in values of cars and also quoted prices of new cars.

- **Newcars.com.** This is part of the family of cars.com.

- **Truecar** gives the range of prices in an area for a particular car (new, used, and certified pre-driven cars).

- **www.autosportcatalog.com.** This is the website of the only catalog that I was able to find. They do carry a wide variety of automotive safety and emergency type items.

- **NEEDS.com.** This is an organization that provides equipment for chemically sensitive patients including possibly gauss meters to measure electromagnetic fields (particularly in hybrids and electric cars), for those who might be interested in that.

- **Eldercare.gov.** (1-800-677-1116). They give information to people who need to acquire transportation if they have lost their driving privileges.

- **Illinois Secretary of State website, Cyberdrive.com.** Provides various services, licensing and registration. Drivers can Google their own states rules of the road or Department of Transportation material. A surprising amount of information is available on the Internet.

- **www.theglobeandmail.com/globe.drive.** Latest auto news, vehicle reviews, photo galleries and car specifications. (Canadian website)

- **mycardoeswhat.org.** This website explains all of the newer safety features, some of which would lead to semi-autonomous and even eventually autonomous cars. This is one of the better websites for this subject and the graphics and explanations are very good.
- **AMA Guide for Older Drivers**, this is now called "Assessing and Counseling Older Drivers." You can also just search the AMA website. This is created in cooperation with NHTSA, and it includes self tests.
- **UMTRI** is the University of Michigan Transportation Research Institute website. They have information on senior mobility, young drivers, automated technology as well as others areas. They do much crash testing, especially applicable to older adults. They utilize advanced technological features and tools. They are designing more realistic crash test dummies. They have a driving decisions workbook which is evaluation of self-screening to assist older drivers in making good decisions regarding safe mobility. They are involved in a global opportunity to improve the safety, mobility, and quality of life of older adults by designing vehicles and technologies that help overcome common age-related deficits. They are involved in a wide spectrum of developing improvements leading to safer driving, including for older drivers. They did an extensive study in 2012 in collaboration with Toyota which showed that driver distraction as shown by parents, even without any verbal exchange, was observed and copied by their children when they became drivers. This is a great resource for anyone in traffic engineering or highway institute schools.
- **Legalcars.com** describes the criteria that one will use to determine whether their car is legal for street use.
- **Carconnection.com**, a website for new and used cars, reviews and other.
- **Drivingschools.com** will bring you to a number of driving schools across the country, some of which can recreate hazardous situations such as ice and snow to better teach the response to those conditions such as one might encounter in Colorado or other mountain states.

- **The American Academy of Orthopedic Surgeons**. They have studies on public education, including at times auto safety advice.
- **The American Academy of Pediatrics**. They have occasionally published studies on infant, child, and adolescent safety in regards to automotive injuries.
- **Ralph Nader.** Ralph Nader is an activist and author of *"Unsafe at any Speed,"* and other books on driving safety. He was one of the activists in the 60's who was the first to call attention to major safety problems in certain cars.
- **DriveChicago.**com, a website for new and used cars, and reviews, especially in the Chicago area.
- **Trafficwaves.**org, a website of William J. Beaty that explains traffic waves(flow) and how an average speed, a safe interval behind the car in front of you, and letting other drivers enter that space, avoids the wave of stopping and starting, and lessens traffic jams without significantly increasing your travel time. The graphics and video are excellent. I highly recommend visiting this website.

ADDITIONAL REFERENCES:

"The Driving Challenge (Learn to be safer and happier on the road)" by Phil Berardelli.

"Safe Young Drivers, A Guide for Parents and Teens" by Phil Berardelli, Nautilus Communications, Inc., P.O. Box 1600, Vienna, VA 22183-1600. Amazon.com may also carry both books which are well written and very useful books to read.

"Crash-Proof Your Kids (Make your teen a safer, smarter driver) "by Timothy C. Smith, Published by Simon and Shuster also possibly available through Amazon.com

"110 Car and Driving Emergencies and How to Survive Them" by James Joseph. Lyons Press, P.O. Box 480, Gilford, CT 06437 is the publisher. In the past, this has also been available through Amazon.com, and may still be.

GLOSSARY

Many of the terms that would ordinarily be in a glossary were adequately explained in the text of *Sane Driving in a Mad World* in conjunction with their usage. The terms that may be important when purchasing a new car, especially with advanced safety features, are mostly described in this section.

Anti-Lock Braking Systems (ABS): An ABS system helps prevent wheels from locking up. When you feel the vibration, just keep pushing, don't let up. This system uses a computer to pump the brakes, keeping the car from locking up and skidding. If you take a curve too fast, or on an icy, slippery road, it helps you to maintain control of the car. It probably does not significantly decrease your stopping distance. It has been around for a number of years and is a very important component of safety.

Adaptive Cruise Control (ACC): This maintains your set speed, your following distance as well. Adaptive Cruise Control does limited braking and you need to know to what extent it can do this. This is not to be confused with automatic emergency braking, or automatic emergency braking alert. Set the desired speed and desired following distance determined by seconds. If the car ahead of you turns off the road, your car may speed up so don't be alarmed by that. Sometimes the distance or seconds for the interval is referred to as gap. It generally only works above 25 mph.

Back-Up Camera: There have been marked improvements in back-up cameras in terms of sunlight not making it difficult to read, and also being easier to estimate distances, with grid-lines. Back-up cameras have been around for a number of years and will be required in all new cars by 2018.

They are activated when the car is put in reverse. The lens can be obscured by dirt, snow, or even direct sunlight. It is not a substitute for looking in your rearview mirror and your side mirrors as well, and over your shoulder through the back window as you back up slowly. Usually the display screen is found on the center console or the center part of the dashboard, or may be found in other parts of the car easily visible to the driver. Back-up cameras may not detect objects close to the rear of the car or under the car.

Rear Cross Traffic Alert: This is one of the newer options being offered on some cars and will alert you to traffic if you are backing up, especially in a parking lot or into a street. It is still important to back-up slowly, looking out the back and side windows and using the rear or side view mirrors until you have a good view.

Automatic Emergency Brake Alert (Sometimes called Forward Collision Warning): This will cause a vibration or sound a noise if you need to brake, but is not as useful as automatic emergency braking. Some cars will have both, with the alert first sounding, and then if there is no response, braking will be automatic, up to a certain speed.

Automatic Emergency Braking: This is going to save a number of lives and reduce injuries and damages and is becoming more widely available as an option and may soon become mandatory. It is important to know at what speeds it is operative since the early versions were operative at low speeds and subsequently the operative speed has been elevated considerably. Automatic emergency braking may not always prevent a rear end collision, but at least it will make it less severe. You should still brake or steer to avoid the hazard ahead.

Lane Departure Warning: Lane Departure Warning may not work if the lane lines are covered or faded, although newer techniques using GPS might eventually compensate for that. Again nothing is as important as an alert and focused driver. The turn signal overrides the lane departure warning. A more advanced system, Lane Keeping Assist will actually nudge the car back into the lane if you are just drifting. Lane Departure Warning and Lane Keeping Assist are designed more for highway driving.

Adaptive Headlights: These headlights swivel the headlights as you turn the steering wheel going around a curve increasing the visibility. HIL or High Intensity Lights and also LED's may provide better illumination. There are also self-adjusting headlights that go to high beam when there are no oncoming cars and then go back down when there are. Adaptive headlights also adjust to going over hills.

Blind Spot Monitoring: This feature will be helpful, but again still a focused and alert driver with their mirrors set properly and who looks out the windows, is hard to compete with. Blind spot monitor may not detect motorcycles or very slow or fast moving vehicles and can be blocked by fog, ice or snow. Blind spot monitors will warn you when a car enters your blind spot on either side, if there is a car next to you may hear a warning or see a blinking icon if you engage your turn signal. As this is developed, including pedestrian and bicycle detection, it may enhance driving safety. This is not a substitute for careful driving and lane change habits, but is in addition.

Automatic Parallel Parking and Parking Sensors: This has been available for a few years on a number of cars, and some are also able to tell you if there is sufficient space, and will back the car into the space, but you may still have to brake and pull forward or back-up, although some newer versions may incorporate those actions as well. Automatic parallel parking may not brake or automatically shift gears, but newer versions might.

Pedestrian Detection: This alerts the driver and automatically brakes if there is a pedestrian in the path, especially at speeds around 20 to 25 mph.

Push Button Start/Stop: In most instances where there is a push button start or stop, the button actually has that written on it, i.e. Engine Start/Stop. The brake has to be applied and the gear in Park or clutch-in if it is a stick shift, to start. For stopping, push the stop button and step on the brake pedal.

Tire Pressure Monitoring System (TPMS): This is a system which will alert you on your instrument panel with an icon if one or more tires are 25% below the recommended inflation level. This has been around for at least 10 years, if not longer, and has cut down on the number of accidents due to tire failure. TPM may also alert you with a change of seasons, warmer to colder, or change of elevation, and usually doesn't specify which of the tires needs attention. Some versions will show which tire or tires are under-inflated. In some cars it may also appear for over-inflation. It is not a substitute for carefully checking tire pressure periodically, at least monthly, and also noting the tire condition on a walk-around each time you get into your car.

Drowsiness Alert: Alerts you if you are drowsy and suggests you take a break; it may show up with a cup of coffee or other symbol appearing on your dash. This does not steer you back into your lane.

Electronic Stability Control (ESC): Helps prevent loss of control in curves and emergency steering maneuvers by stabilizing your car when it begins to veer off your intended path,and may or may not prevent a roll over. It is always on. It adjusts braking and gas, can prevent skids and rollovers especially on wet roads, stabilizes cars steering, wheels and direction. It takes control of one or more wheels, adjusts braking and gas in milliseconds. ESC relies on an ABS to function properly. It is less effective on gravel and lightly packed snow. Prevents over steering and under steering by braking individual wheels and reducing engine speed, helping you maintain control.

Traction Control: Supplies power to the wheel that has traction.

The plan is for cars that are autonomous to incorporate most if not all of these above advances plus others that will be forthcoming.

Paddle Shifters: Paddle shifters on both sides of the steering wheel allow you to up or down shift without your hands leaving the steering wheel. There is no clutch needed and this is sometimes called electronic shifting. Currently they are on some makes of cars including some Chrysler Fiat models. The advantage is said to be quicker shifting, but for the average driver, they are probably not an advantage, and sometimes even confusing.

Intelligent Disobedience. This is referring to guide dogs for the blind. The dogs are taught to go in front of cars, but when the car has stopped too far into or past the crosswalk, they will use "Intelligent Disobedience" and go around the back of the car.

Culvert. Usually a large pipe, at least several feet in diameter, underneath a road to allow the passage of water. It may be partially embedded in soil and this is considered to be a safer shelter than staying in the car during a tornado, if it is not too filled with water.

Speeding. Exceeding the posted speed limit or going too fast for conditions (weather, road, and driver).

Covering the brake. This means having your foot at least on the brake pedal even if not depressing it, as you approach an intersection, and as you get into the intersection, switching it to the gas pedal, especially if you need to get out of the intersection quickly.

Department of Transportation (D.O.T.) The department of each state that has to do with regulations regarding vehicle and highway maintenance.

In The Future:

V2V (Vehicle to Vehicle): An article by Joan Lowy of the Associated Press, in the *Chicago Tribune* on Sunday August 28, 2016 mentioned that vehicle to vehicle communication, called V2V, might be available in the fairly near future. "With V2V, cars and trucks wirelessly transmit their location, speed, direction, and other information ten times per second. The hope is that this will prevent crashes. V2V's range is up to 1,000 yards in all directions, even when sightlines are blocked by buildings or other obstacles." According to the article, this gives the advantage of being able to detect a potential collision before the driver can see the threat, unlike the sensors in cameras of self driving cars that will only note what is immediately around the vehicle. This article also indicates that they predict that V2V may prevent up to 80% of collisions that don't involve an impaired driver. Other advantages may be in terms of expediting traffic. Realistically Ms. Lowy points out that it could be more then 20 years before the full benefits of V2V are appreciated, mainly because it takes decades for the automotive fleet to be completely replaced, or even if this will all be implemented.

APPENDIX

IN GRADE SCHOOL, I WAS A crossing guard, which might have been some indication of a developing interest. My own driving experience spans over six decades of serious accident-free driving, partly luck, and partly because of the approach detailed in *Sane Driving in a Mad World*. During my third year as a pre-medical student at the University of Denver, I had access to a car, and besides driving to and from school, during Christmas break, at age 18, I drove from Denver to Kansas City by myself. Although I didn't think of this as being unusual or dangerous, my parents were not too thrilled about this unannounced trip. My father insisted on driving back to Denver with me. On the way back through Kansas, luckily right in front of a filling station, smoke began coming out of the front of the car. It turned out to be a broken fan belt, which was quickly replaced, and the rest of the trip was uneventful.

During the summer before entering the Feinberg School of Medicine of Northwestern University in Chicago, I worked as a laborer in the Denver City and County Mountain Parks system. During my three years in school in Denver, borrowing my cousin's car, I drove into the mountains, especially the front range, very frequently. I also, during that time drove my cousin's panel truck, mostly to pick up ice for their restaurant, as well as for other errands. During the summer between my first and second year at medical school, I drove a tractor with a six foot weed cutter blade, again for the City and County of Denver, for three weeks. At that point, I was able to get a transfer back to working in the mountains, which I enjoyed so much. While in Denver, I also was the sole teacher for a favorite cousin, regarding learning to drive.

During the summer between my second and third year in medical school, I drove a Checker Taxicab, in Chicago. This was a longer model, no longer made, with two jump seats in the back, along with the rear seat.

I, and my wife Marsha, have helped our two sons and our grandson, Jake, to learn to drive, along with their driver's education and/or private driver's school lessons. I look forward to being a part of the learning to drive experience of our other grandchildren, Jordaan and Nicole. I hope that *Sane Driving in a Mad World* will augment and reinforce their natural tendency to be courteous, responsible, and safe, as is their brother Jake, our son, Stephen (their father), our daughter-in-law, Lisa (their mother), and our other son, Richard.

I took a course in motorcycle riding at Northeastern University in Chicago. There I learned how vulnerable motorcyclists are, and why it is so important for automobile drivers to monitor their mirrors and be aware of their approaching presence.

I have driven in most of the states in the Continental U.S.A., including most of our major cities. I have driven extensively in Chicago; Kansas City, Missouri (my hometown); Overland Park, Kansas; Denver, Colorado; Cincinnati, Ohio (my wife Marsha's hometown); and in the suburbs surrounding those cities. I'm most familiar with Illinois, Wisconsin, Indiana, Michigan, Iowa, Missouri, Kansas, Colorado, New Mexico, Florida, and California. I have also driven in Hawaii, Puerto Rico, and many parts of Europe, including a stretch on the Autobahn from Basel, Switzerland, up the Rhine River to Cologne, Germany, and then on to Brussels, Belgium. I've driven in Canada, especially in the northwest mountainous sections, and also in Vancouver, as well as Victoria.

When I traveled by plane to more distant cities for medical meetings, I would often rent a car, and spend some extra time before or after the meetings to visit areas of interest nearby. My wife and our sons sometimes accompanied me on these trips, as well as on numerous other trips. I estimate that I probably have driven either close to or over one million miles, and I find that almost daily, I notice and learn something new.

My interest in preventative medicine, which would include helping patients avoid serious injuries, and even saving lives, extends into the laborious and detailed preparation of *Sane Driving in a Mad World*. My goal in writing *Sane Driving in a Mad World* is to help both drivers and passengers achieve a safer and more comfortable driving experience. I also hope that the safety of pedestrians will be enhanced.

Treat others as you would like to be treated by them, by driving safely, courteously, and responsibly. Help to make this mad world saner, at least in regards to driving.

Robert W. Boxer, M.D.

INDEX

Printed in the United States
By Bookmasters